MW01073295

Business Leadership and Diversity

Jason Miller

Foreword by Dr. Julie Ducharme

Introduction by Reggie Walker,
Former NFL All-Star

Chris O'Byrne,
Patricia Baronowski-Schneider,
Ira Bowman, Dr. Julie Ducharme,
Lynn Hoerauf, Brianna Jackson,
Mike Jackson, Ryan Jackson,
Michael Markiewicz, Dr. Bruce Rippee,
and Luba Sakharuk

ISBN: 978-1-957217-22-2 (hardback)

ISBN: 978-1-957217-21-5 (paperback)

ISBN: 978-1-957217-23-9 (ebook)

CONTENTS

FOREWORD

Dr. Julie Ducharme

Every child dreams of becoming important someday. When I ask my own children what they want to be when they grow up, they say doctor, firefighter, police officer, or astronaut. When you are a kid, there are no limits to what your dreams can be. I remember I wanted to be everything from a mermaid to a superhero, journalist, ESPN correspondent, and Olympic athlete. In those moments of dreaming as a child, no one ever said I couldn't do that job because of my gender, ethnicity, or religious beliefs. They let me dream of the possibilities.

When I think of the words *different*, *diversity*, and *authenticity*, the first person who comes to mind is someone who was born very frail and was not expected to live to adulthood. In fact, at the age of two, her mother was accused of a crime and beheaded. The young girl was declared a bastard child and sent to live in exile. She had many things going against her. She found herself in a poor position, but fate is an interesting thing.

When she was twenty-five, this young woman became one of the most prominent and powerful world leaders. That woman was Queen Elizabeth I. She was a unique, diverse leader who brought diversity and authenticity into a world that thought you should be beheaded if you were different.

One of the first expectations of Queen Elizabeth was to get married to royalty from another country to bring peace to their lands and for her to give birth to have a successor. The philosophy of that time was that women didn't rule kingdoms, they birthed men who did. But Elizabeth knew if she married someone from a foreign country, she would lose all her power and then someone would run the country who didn't know or love the country like she did.

Queen Elizabeth knew she needed to save England that was rapidly going downhill since her father had run it into the ground. She broke all the rules, and she brought in diversity in a way that no one had ever thought of. She didn't know everything at age twenty-five, but she surrounded herself with the brightest and the best minds. She connected with the people, and she became their beloved queen. She rode into battles in armor and broke all the rules that queens typically had to live by.

This audacious and diverse leadership style left England as one of the most powerful countries in the world upon her death. Elizabeth showed them that women could lead, women had the mental capacity to run countries, and even though how Elizabeth led differed from all the expected cultural norms, her leadership worked. People still study Queen Elizabeth and her diverse leadership style and tactics. Researchers and scholars agree that her diversity of thought, diversity of leadership, and diversity of character brought success to England. Her unique approaches have long stood the test of time, as many in our modern world look to her for inspiration for integrating diversity within various facets of an organization.

For the last one hundred years, women have attempted to redefine themselves from the traditional female stereotypes that have followed us for so long. At first, I thought diversity meant only cultural diversity, but early in my career I realized that diversity encompassed diversity of thought, diversity of skills, and diversity of people, which all lead to something that changed the industry—innovation! I was a mere twenty-three years old when I stepped into the position of college professor and the head coach of the college volleyball program. Despite winning national titles, and already having both a bachelor's and master's degree, I quickly realized I was one of the few women in these departments, and my youth and gender were not the most popular among the older male professors and coaches. The male coaches didn't like that they had to be "appropriate" around me now that there was a female coach. Instead of embracing my experience, they were intimated by me because I had accomplished so much at such an early age. They treated me as an outcast. The other professors thought I was too young to teach or be a master in my industry, and they all suggested I had slept my way into the position. No one really wanted me around. It was my first-time facing issues with diversity specific to my gender and age.

I was raised with a "you can do anything" motto from my parents, and I naively thought I could go do anything. It didn't occur to me that people would have issues with my age, gender, or even my thought processes. But there I was in an interview for a full-time business professorship position and the person interviewing me said, "Sweetheart, the English department is down the hall. Women don't do business." At that moment, I owned two successful businesses that I had started in my early twenties.

A well-intentioned older woman told me I needed to fit in. She said I shouldn't try to be different and should dress and act like the men so they would hassle me less. I actually tried that. I bought a black suit, put my hair in a bun, and kept my mouth shut at all meetings. I quickly realized this was not helping me or the organization. I needed to be my authentic self, which meant that I needed to help diversify people's thoughts on women in leadership positions and women in the business industry that was mostly male driven. I had to be an authentic leader and show them that different wasn't bad, different was just—different—and different could still be good.

I could give you a long list of companies that have treated different as bad. But I could also give you a long list of companies that have embraced different, such as Google, Apple, and Zappos, to name a few. They embrace differences, they embrace change, they embrace innovation, and what they have created was spectacular. How often do companies find themselves ignorant of how to approach diversity and inclusion in the workplace? Change is never easy, ask any leader who has tried to bring substantial change. But change is essential for today's organizations to create a competitive advantage with a diverse workforce, not just diversity in ethnicity, but also in thought, skills, and leadership. The first and most challenging aspect of embracing diversity is to define it in your organization. I challenge you to work together to meet this goal.

Introduction

BY
Reggie Walker, Former NFL All-Star

Welcome to our book on driving organizational impact through diversity. I'm excited to share our experiences of success through embracing diversity and creating an inclusive workplace.

As a former NFL all-star, I understand the importance of creating an inviting and supportive environment to maximize success. My teams achieved great success when we could come together as a unified group, despite our differences, with a common goal in mind.

In this book, we provide insights on how to leverage diversity to create positive and sustainable change in organizations. We discuss how to create a culture of inclusion, how to celebrate diversity, and how to leverage a diverse workforce for maximum benefit.

We also delve into the importance of developing a diversity mindset that encourages and supports people from all backgrounds. We provide advice on the golden rule of diversity and how to hire on merit and not only diversity. Finally, we provide insight into how to innovate and succeed through diversity.

Diversity is essential for any organization that wants to move forward and be successful in today's global economy. It's essential for organizations to create a culture of inclusion and acceptance that allows people from different backgrounds to work together and bring a unique perspective to any problem. Organizational success largely depends on the ability to build strong teams that are diverse and inclusive. Organizations must create a culture where employees feel respected and appreciated and where everyone is encouraged to bring their unique perspectives to the table.

This book provides advice on how to celebrate diversity and how to leverage a diverse workforce for maximum benefit. We also discuss how to create a culture of inclusion and how to develop a diversity mindset.

The importance of the golden rule of diversity is essential for any organization that wants to move forward and be successful. This rule states everyone should be treated equally, regardless of their background or identity. This means that everyone should be respected and appreciated for their unique contributions to the organization.

In addition to the golden rule, organizations must also hire on merit and not on diversity. This means that candidates should be judged on their qualifications and experience, not on their race, gender, or other personal characteristics. By doing this, organizations can ensure that they are hiring the most qualified individuals and creating an inclusive workplace.

Finally, organizations must also innovate through diversity. This means that they should be open to new ideas and perspectives from different backgrounds and cultures. This can help to create new and innovative solutions to problems and help organizations stay competitive in the global economy.

This book provides insight into how to create a culture of inclusion and respect, how to leverage a diverse workforce, how to hire on merit, and how to innovate through diversity. We also discuss the importance of celebrating diversity and developing a diversity mindset. By following the advice in this book, organizations can create an environment that encourages and supports diversity and ultimately drive organizational impact.

Creating an inclusive workplace is essential for any organization that wants to be successful. It's important to recognize the value of different backgrounds and perspectives and to create an environment where everyone can feel safe, respected, and appreciated.

I hope you find this book helpful in your journey to create a culture of inclusion and respect. By embracing diversity and creating an inclusive workplace, organizations can be successful in the global economy. Thank you for taking the time to learn more about the importance of diversity and inclusion.

Driving Organizational Impact

Jason Miller

From our businesses to our homes, discovering how to lead a diversity-centered life has quickly become one of the most important topics for businesses in any industry. By recognizing and appreciating individual differences and commonalities, those who strive for a successful career understand that embracing diversity and influencing positive change in our communities can make all the difference in our success. But, regardless of size or purpose, all businesses face unique challenges while working toward their personal goals. This is where leadership and diversity come together to create authentic and impactful results as the first step toward a business shift and creative solutions for change.

Through mindful diversity initiatives across all levels of business, you can transform individuals into a strong collective by tapping into the different strengths and lived experiences of the people engaged in our work. These can be our employees, customers, professional communities, or even those who mentor us. These strengths and experiences can guide your business and entrepreneurial goals toward further innovation while creating lasting change that reflects the diversity of our workforce and the communities we serve. As you aim to meet the growing demand for diversity-focused businesses, you first must understand what it means to be a leader in today's world and understand diversity at its core. You will only learn to exercise effective leadership strategies when you clearly understand both. Understanding the connection between strong leadership and diversity will not come without challenges, doubts, and many questions. Discomfort is a vital part of any effective change. Still, leading with diversity as a core value will help you and your business foster successful relationships with communities and customers.

Leadership encompasses much more than taking charge and having a vision; it involves developing relationships and empowering people from all walks of life. To be successful at developing these relationships, you must learn about different life perspectives and lived experiences, which requires you to be curious about the world around you and the lives that people live in and outside of their professional roles. The important thing about enlisting a tool like curiosity is that curiosity exists without judgment. It directs us to learn and absorb new information that would help us to live in the experiences of others for a moment and to understand human behavior better. These new perspectives can then help us, as leaders, form solutions that meet the needs of our business in ways that we may have never been able to conceptualize on our own or based on our own lived and limited experiences. That's the beauty of the role of a leader. Leaders can create better when they can expand the limitations of their creativity and understanding of the world. Being curious leaders will help us run, build, and create better businesses with progressive business practices that reflect the vibrancy of our communities.

Being a leader also means being a role model in your business community. Every decision to improve your business practices will inspire other business owners, entrepreneurs, and aspiring business professionals to follow suit. You will naturally empower and encourage others when you proudly show your commitment to learning about new experiences and diverse perspectives. With this wisdom, you will be able to instill confidence in others and help them reach their greatest business potential and contributions. This process not only supports innovation and overall customer morale but also garners support for you as a leader as you actively create the safety and opportunity for others to be the dynamic and diverse individuals they are. Modeling these values can positively impact how people visit, purchase, or invest in your business or dream. After all, allowing people to be seen and appreciated for who they are authentically is the key to cultivating a thriving business community and approach. Shifting your leadership style this way requires intelligence, self-awareness, creativity, and compassion. This type of leadership creates an environment where individuals feel respected, which is a vital element at the heart of what solid leadership is all about.

In addition to leading with curiosity, good leaders understand the importance of embracing diversity, including differences in gender, ability, race, ethnicity, opinion, and experience. Diversity is the inclusion of people of different races, cultures, etc., in a group or organization. And while diversity is not enough for a complete cultural overhaul, centering and prioritizing diversity in everything from marketing to product selection to customer service is the best first step to making a meaningful change in the lives of others and yourself. Today's changing world requires us to be open-minded and actively seek different perspectives from diverse backgrounds. Success can be found and achieved through centering diversity and strong leadership skills.

Diversity is beautiful, representing the many hues of nature and the great spectrum of humanity that creates our grand tapestry. Not only does it result in stunning imagery to feast our eyes upon, but diversity offers tangible benefits, too. When we embrace different cultures, beliefs, and points of view, we gain new perspectives on life and fresh insights into our own. By collaborating with others from varied backgrounds, we can innovate more quickly and purposefully, solving problems through collective genius. But most importantly, when we come together from disparate walks of life, we learn empathy; welcoming differences allows us to find common ground and discover more deeply all that makes us human.

Working together across different life experiences is a priceless experience. We can come together in understanding and com-passion by recognizing each other's individualities. It could be something as simple as a difference in background or view on what success looks like. No matter the divide, when we come together and tap into our shared humanity, amazing things can happen. Diversity brings an array of perspectives and ideas that help us better relate to each other and build bridges between ideas. In a business setting, this ability to look beyond the facade of background or status opens up possibilities we couldn't see before. It allows us to develop business solutions that are robust and comprehensive, understanding that, at the core, those things that make us both different and alike will enable us to accomplish great things.

While diversity is beautiful and essential all on its own, pair-ing it with business can result in a powerful combination.

Companies that commit to celebrating diversity often reap the rewards like fresh perspectives, innovative ideas, and better problem-solving skills. Fostering an environment that celebrates diversity can also improve communication among team members, leading to higher engagement and morale levels. In the long term, creating diverse teams can benefit businesses by bringing in an array of viewpoints centered on customer satisfaction and the bottom line. When more companies are willing to embrace difference, they'll be open to a fascinating suite of opportunities that take their business forward into success.

When it comes to success, being a successful leader in today's diverse business sphere requires strength of character and an expansive worldview. The key to success lies in embracing the unique qualities of everyone around you, regardless of age, race, gender, or sexual orientation. By being open-minded and valuing the different perspectives offered by each individual in your organization, it is possible to make the most of your differences and unify them with a common goal. Furthermore, influential leaders know that listening is just as critical, if not more so, than speaking up. They recognize the power of gathering input from all their employees before making decisions based on this collective wisdom. Finally, having an absolute commitment to diversity creates the foundation for a strong culture of trust, fostering improved collaboration and encouraging diversity within all levels of the company.

Becoming an effective leader also requires a deep understanding of the modern world and, in particular, the importance of diversity. Effective leadership means appreciating different perspectives and experiences and understanding different cultural contexts. It also means going the extra mile to learn more about the community your business serves, your employees' backgrounds, and your vendor's commitment to diversity. With this knowledge, leaders can foster cultures of inclusion that impact the roots of the business, not just at its surface level. Addressing diversity needs at their roots will create a more enjoyable atmosphere and capitalize on employees' talents and the community's diverse visions. An effective leader can nurture such an environment, allowing new ideas to flourish and everyone to reach their fullest potential. By learning how to do this, leaders can reap the benefits of a successful diversified workforce and business ethos.

Establishing and maintaining a diverse workplace can be an incredible asset for any business. It is essential that, as a business, you can ensure that your policies, practices, and culture encourage a sense of diverse perspectives, ideas, and opinions that reflect the business community as a whole. Being proactive in this area, such as by creating training programs focused on breaking down all forms of discrimination, will go a long way in improving employee satisfaction and fostering creativity. Equipping your business with mentoring opportunities, diversity dashboard tools, and equal and equitable opportunities across the board will ensure that you are centering diversity needs in your industry. Incorporating these steps will lead you in the right direction and naturally support a diversity-centered workplace and value system. Although it takes effort to create an atmosphere of unity and acceptance within an organization, it can immensely benefit employers, employees, and the business community.

When forming a diverse business, it's essential to start by emphasizing the value of inclusivity. An understanding that every individual brings something unique and invaluable to the team should be at the core of any successful organization. After all, diversity in experience and backgrounds leads to more innovative ideas and a broader potential for success. You'll want to build a staff of professionals willing to share different perspectives, collaborate, and open the door for creativity to thrive. Incorporating these qualities will require staff and a workplace culture that values empathy and an openness to learning new perspectives and trusting people's lived realities as valid for them. Lastly, create a culture where everyone feels safe expressing themselves and doing whatever it takes to get the job done without fear of repercussion. Embrace each person's differences while ensuring they have access to the same opportunities within your organization.

Although the steps seem easy enough, actually implementing this change around diversity will be challenging. It can, at times, require a huge shift in mindset and strategy, which is a heavy lift for anyone. Business leaders who strive for diversity face various challenges in achieving their goals. One common issue is convincing their peers to recognize and close any existing disparities between genders, ethnicities, and other traits. Bridging divides between genders, ethnicities, and other protected classes in business is a challenging feat that requires dedication, passion, and creative problem-solving to be successful. It's essential to take the time to consider the opinions of all stakeholders involved and ensure they are taken into account before you make business decisions. To truly make an impact, businesses must craft solutions that recognize existing disparities and actively create efforts to close these gaps with meaningful progress. Change is likely to be incremental, but with an effective strategy for identifying, understanding, and closing these disparities, everyone involved can work together to center diversity for everyone.

An additional challenge may be finding ways to intentionally include individuals from communities that have been historically and institutionally marginalized and who may not typically have access to business mentoring or work in your particular industry. Bringing individuals from these communities into positions of authority can create a comprehensive understanding of different perspectives within the organization and help lead diversity from the top down. Furthermore, business leaders must ensure that hiring policies are fair and effective at providing opportunities for people of all ages and backgrounds so that fresh perspectives can flourish within the business. Moving beyond traditional structures in hiring practices and leadership decisions can present the opportunity to create, build and sustain a diverse business community rooted in an open-minded culture where possibility meets inspiration.

Diversity in leadership and business is vital to any thriving and progressive business or entrepreneurial endeavor. After all, when we work together with people who are different from ourselves, we create something more significant than the sum of its parts. With each unique perspective and set of experiences, new ideas emerge that have the potential to open up new opportunities for growth and development. When a company allows its business to embrace diversity within its workplace values and with its customer base, an environment is created where success can flourish on multiple levels, and everyone has the chance to contribute in meaningful ways. Valuing diversity and the cultures that make our world so diverse isn't just crucial regarding ethical responsibilities. Centering diversity is critical to achieving innovation and prosperity that drives business progress.

Culture is a lens through which we can understand the vibrant diversity of different people and ideas. The structures we create to mediate between us - language, art, music, food – break down the communication barriers that divide us. In perfect alignment, the industries our businesses and entrepreneurship touch, contribute to each of these ways of cultural and diverse connection. By getting to know each other's cultures, appreciating one another's values, and sharing our stories, every aspect of life benefits and becomes enriched. We're all on a journey to learn more about ourselves and others by understanding our differences and how to incorporate the diversity of our world into what we do. In this sense, diversity has never been more critical in this fantastic variety and complexity world. By connecting with the common threads woven into our collective identity, cultures, and lived experiences, we can take confident steps toward building better business communities for all.

In the ever-changing and increasingly competitive business world, diversity is essential in creating a vibrant and inclusive workplace, which can help a business to thrive. It allows organizations to develop solutions, strategies, and initiatives that are all the more effective by being influenced by those with different backgrounds and perspectives. This support network not only expands the range of ideas and actions circulating within the company but also bolsters morale among employees and customers to help create an environment where each individual feels valued for their unique contribution. Diversity in business is advantageous economically and is conducive to personal growth. Centering diversity in your industry will have lasting benefits that can deliver real, long-term, and sustainable change in the business world.

There are many reasons to make diversity a central part of your business model. Doing so can improve team dynamics, reflect and connect with your customer base, foster new perspectives and creativity, and much more. When it comes to success in business, diversity is key. As we continue to see the business world change and grow, it's more important than ever to have diverse voices in leadership positions. With various perspectives, businesses can make better decisions and even avoid major business pitfalls. Now is the time to start if you still need to incorporate diversity into your business. Centering and integrating diversity will help your business succeed like never before.

DIVERSITY AND BUSINESS LEADERSHIP

CHRIS O'BYRNE

D iversity and business leadership are two critical elements of organizational success in today's globalized and rapidly changing business environment. Diversity in the workplace refers to the range of differences among people in an organization, including differences in race, gender, age, sexual orientation, religion, and other characteristics. Business leadership, on the other hand, refers to the ability of individuals and teams to effectively manage and guide organizations in pursuit of their goals and objectives. Together, diversity and business leadership play a vital role in driving organizational success and innovation and are essential for organizations to remain competitive in today's rapidly changing business environment.

One of the most significant benefits of diversity in the workplace is that it can lead to increased creativity and innovation. When people with different backgrounds, perspectives, and experiences come together to work on a common goal, they bring a wide range of ideas and approaches that can lead to new and innovative solutions. This is especially important in today's fast-paced business environment, where organizations are constantly seeking new ways to stay ahead of the competition and meet the changing needs of customers. Moreover, diversity brings different cultural and educational backgrounds that can be useful in approaching and understanding the global market and anticipating customer needs.

Another crucial benefit of diversity in the workplace is that it can lead to increased productivity and performance. Studies have shown that diverse teams tend to be more effective and efficient than homogenous teams and that individuals from diverse backgrounds tend to be more motivated and engaged in their work. This can lead to improved organizational performance and productivity and ultimately benefit the bottom line. Furthermore, diverse teams tend to have more open communication and better problem-solving skills, which can lead to more effective decision-making.

However, for organizations to fully realize the benefits of diversity in the workplace, effective business leadership is essential. Leaders play a vital role in creating and fostering a culture of diversity and inclusion and in ensuring that the benefits of diversity are realized. This requires leaders to be aware of their own biases and actively work to overcome them and to create an environment in which all employees feel valued and respected. Leaders must also ensure that the organization's policies and practices are inclusive and that all employees have equal opportunities to succeed.

One key aspect of effective business leadership in a diverse workplace is the ability to communicate effectively with people from different backgrounds and cultures. This requires leaders to be culturally aware and able to understand and appreciate the perspectives and experiences of people from different backgrounds. It also requires leaders to be able to communicate clearly and effectively with people from different backgrounds and to be able to build trust and understanding. Furthermore, effective communication also means being able to understand the different communication styles of diverse team members and adapt accordingly.

Another vital aspect of effective business leadership in a diverse workplace is the ability to manage and lead diverse teams. This requires leaders to be able to understand and appreciate the different perspectives and experiences of team members and to be able to effectively manage and lead teams that are diverse in terms of race, gender, age, sexual orientation, and other characteristics. It also requires leaders to be able to build trust and understanding among team members and to be able to effectively resolve conflicts and manage differences. In addition, effective leadership in diverse teams also means being able to recognize and address microaggressions and promoting an environment of respect and dignity for all team members.

Creating and maintaining a diverse and inclusive workplace culture is crucial for organizations looking to leverage the benefits of diversity. A positive workplace culture that values and respects diversity can lead to increased employee engagement, improved morale, and higher retention rates. This can lead to a more productive and efficient workforce, which ultimately benefits the bottom line. Furthermore, a diverse and inclusive culture can also attract a wider pool of talented and qualified candidates.

A positive workplace culture that values and respects diversity can lead to increased employee engagement, improved morale, and higher retention rates. This can lead to a more productive and efficient workforce, which ultimately benefits the bottom line. Additionally, an inclusive culture can attract and retain top talent and can also improve the organization's reputation in the community and among customers.

Moreover, diversity in leadership also plays a crucial role in shaping the culture of an organization. When leaders come from diverse backgrounds, they bring different perspectives and experiences to the table, which can lead to a more inclusive and innovative culture. This can lead to better decision-making and ultimately benefit the organization. Furthermore, a diverse leadership team can provide role models and mentors for diverse employees and can also help to break down barriers and stereotypes within the organization.

Despite the many benefits of diversity and inclusion in the workplace, organizations still face many challenges in creating and maintaining a diverse and inclusive culture. Some of the most common challenges include unconscious bias, lack of representation, and a lack of understanding of the importance of diversity and inclusion. To overcome these challenges, organizations need to take a comprehensive and strategic approach to diversity and inclusion, which includes training and education, creating inclusive policies and practices, and actively working to increase the representation of diverse groups.

In conclusion, diversity and business leadership are two critical components of organizational success in today's rapidly changing business environment. Organizations that are able to effectively leverage the benefits of diversity in the workplace and that are able to effectively lead and manage diverse teams are more likely to be successful in today's competitive business landscape. Effective business leadership is essential for organizations to be able to fully realize the benefits of diversity in the workplace and for leaders to be able to create and foster a culture of diversity and inclusion. Organizations should actively work to increase diversity and invest in training and education to help leaders and employees understand and appreciate the importance of diversity and inclusion. By embracing diversity and promoting inclusive leadership, organizations can create a more innovative, productive, and successful workforce and ultimately benefit the bottom line.

ABOUT THE AUTHOR

Chris O'Byrne is the CEO of JETLAUNCH Publishing and co-owner of the Strategic Advisor Board and Rogue Publishing Partners. He is also the director of SAB Publishing.

CELEBRATING DIVERSITY

PATRICIA BARONOWSKI-SCHNEIDER

Different backgrounds, lifestyles, social experiences, races, and religions make up diversity and include people, perspectives, topics, and ideas that differ from one another. It is my belief that diversity embraces people of different backgrounds, regardless of their race, geography, experience, gender, or religion. I love learning about different people with different ideas and different backgrounds. I grew up in Manhattan, the melting pot of New York, and truly enjoyed meeting and functioning around such a diverse group of people. I don't like being stuck in the same boring situation all the time. Diversity brings all of this to life. From a scientific point of view, species have a better chance of survival when there is genetic diversity. The ability of a species to adapt and survive is reduced when populations are small and isolated.

I am just one person among billions. It always fascinates me to learn about others. It is how the world evolves. In fact, diversity is part of the natural cycle of evolution. To adapt to change, the population must maintain diversity. Adaptation to changing environments is more likely to happen in populations with greater variability of genes.

My children are also a mixture of diverse nationalities, and my grandchildren expand upon that even more. Even in DNA testing, you can uncover so much diversity in your lifeline you didn't even know existed. Learning about the backgrounds and customs of these nationalities is fascinating to me.

My grandparents immigrated from Poland and Yugoslavia. Learning about the customs and life there helps me to understand more about the life my grandparents had before coming to America. Even the food my grandmother used to cook was different from what I was used to. Going to Polish neighborhoods and eating various foods is a new adventure. In Manhattan alone, there is a food eatery for just about every nationality. Exploring and trying new things brings forth more acceptance and delight.

You may be surprised to learn that over 4,000 religions exist around the world. There are churches, congregations, faith groups, tribes, cultures, and movements that make up these religions. What are the differences? Why does each believe what they believe? Learn about them. Explore and understand how and why some religions think and believe their beliefs. It is helpful to understand this and many other new ideas you can learn from various diversified backgrounds. It doesn't mean that you have to agree with everything you learn, but knowing and understanding the hows and whys helps us to see a little deeper and have more of an understanding of the people we meet.

This is part of how the world evolves. Everything we are today consists of bits and pieces of all that came before us from all over the world. The first humans to arrive in North America approximately 13,000 to 13,500 years ago crossed a land bridge between Asia and Siberia. College students in archaeology learned this in the 1970s. Known collectively as Clovis people, these were the first North Americans.

In my childhood, I was taught the story of how Columbus conquered the Indian lands in America. We are enriched by the stories and backgrounds of people coming from a variety of countries and cultures. It is clear that this will be expanded upon until the end of time.

In addition to guns, iron tools, and weapons, Europeans also brought Christianity and Roman law, sugarcane and wheat, and horses and cattle. Did they know that these technologies and ideas, plants, and animals would transform the lives of Americans?

In addition to establishing the first kindergartens in the United States, German Americans introduced the Christmas tree tradition and popular foods like hot dogs and hamburgers. More than 99% of people with German ancestry have become Americanized, while fewer than 5% speak German.

The written constitution was another ancient Greek concept that influenced the formation of the United States government. The Constitution of the Athenians, along with the laws of many other Greek cities, was compiled and recorded by Aristotle or one of his students.

It was in the 1880s that the Great Migration began when cheap manual labor was needed in America, and convenient immigration laws encouraged this migration. It was during this time when the last Europeans immigrated to America.

I am not technically a history buff. However, I constantly ask why, always wanting to know more, asking questions, and trying to understand why things are the way they are. I am fascinated to learn about diversity and why the world is the way it is. It would be a never-ending project to continually go further back in time to learn more, but my point is that diversity is fundamental. No one person is perfect, and no one person has all the answers. Bringing a bit together from various people, customs, backgrounds, thoughts, and understanding creates a whole new idea. This is how the world grows.

As a result of diversity, people can learn from each other's ideas and experiences. To solve problems effectively, it is important to bring in different ideas and perspectives. Working in diverse teams promotes creativity and dialogue. Diversity is very valuable.

It has been proven that you can boost productivity by 35% by diversifying your team. Having a diverse workforce increases your chances of understanding your customers' needs. Employee morale and productivity will also increase when there is a diversity of opinion in the workplace. Since the world consists of people from different countries, nationalities, backgrounds, and religions, it is beneficial to have a diverse staff of employees who can understand and accommodate such needs and desires. An American from another country could offer insight into a product in ways that I may not have otherwise thought of. This is how new ideas and new products are created and evolve.

I like to ask everyone their thoughts. Maybe you will explain something to me that I didn't know or never thought of. Maybe after hearing it, I will say, "Wow, that is great; I hadn't thought of that," or maybe I will digest what you say and reply, "That is a good idea, however….." and speak about my thoughts on why that may or may not work. We are bouncing ideas off of one another. But the point is that someone else may have a different idea or viewpoint stemming from different backgrounds and upbringing, and that may or may not be valuable. Either way, we share ideas, and either I gain a new understanding and a new idea from this person, or I explain my viewpoint, and they gain a new understanding or a new viewpoint. It's always a win-win.

Creativity is enhanced by diversity. New perspectives and information are sought, leading to better problem-solving and decision-making. Innovation and unfettered discoveries are possible when diversity is embraced by companies.

Every business should know that we need to evolve and grow with the changing times. Being creative and innovative is essential to standing out and making your mark. For example, if I have a skincare product and am marketing that to customers in the United States, I may have employees from Asia, Europe, etc., along with some who believe in "all natural" or who have other ideas from their upbringing and environment. I once saw a skin cream made from bee venom. They state that when applied, bee venom cream penetrates your skin, increasing your blood circulation and production of collagen and elastin. As a result, your skin looks plumper and firmer, lifting, filling, and smoothing out fine lines and wrinkles. To be honest, as a native New Yorker, I would never ever have even thought of this. Bees are not a big thing in a city, so it is not something I have major exposure to, so how would I have known this?

I also see many Asian skincare routines online. If you search, you will see routines for just about every nationality out there. When you see other people from other cultures with great skin, healthy lifestyles, or living longer, it makes us curious to know what their secrets are. This is why having people from all backgrounds brings new ideas to businesses, along with new ideas for your business and products for your customers.

New ideas and inputs are added to a diverse workplace. As a result of this diversity of talent, employees have a greater variety of skills and experiences. This increases the potential for increased productivity. Creativity increases when cultures from different backgrounds come together.

Let's say, for example, that you worked in a restaurant and were trained in one way of making food. Along comes someone from another country who has their own training in making food. Here again, they offer their advice and opinion, and you offer yours. Chances are there is a happy medium there that benefits everyone in the end, and a new system is born.

This can be hard for people who are technically thick-headed and not willing to listen or change. I know some people who believe things should be their way or no way, and they are not willing to listen or change. That is unfortunate. The world is always changing and evolving, and you must be on board. I am not suggesting you change your ways 100%; I am suggesting you at least listen and learn from others. You never know how taking a few pieces of information here and there and incorporating them into your current plan of action can change things for the better. It never hurts to try. We must be on board the train of life and ride the waves of change. What better way to learn than from those around us.

It is through diversity that we gain a variety of perspectives. A team is more likely to be innovative and solve problems when members come from different backgrounds, cultures, and experiences. Results can be thoroughly vetted as a result of this. Additionally, leaders are more likely to be able to make informed decisions.

To form acceptance, we must learn and understand. Again, this doesn't mean that you have to agree with everything, but at least try to learn and understand. For example, every Muslim is obligated to pray five times a day: Fajr, Zuhr, Asr, Maghrib, and Isha. The prayer called Salah is prayed in the congregation every day at dawn, post noon, during the evening, at the evening, and at night. Now, as a Catholic, I do not do this, but that doesn't mean that I have any right to judge or comment. This is their belief system. Once I understand this, I can accept that this practice is taking place and allow them their time and space to pray.

Knowing and understanding various backgrounds helps us accept diversity. Various other cultures may not agree with or support my beliefs and customs, and that is okay. I always use the term, "We can agree to disagree." Sadly, some people say, "If they don't like it, then they shouldn't have come to this country." That is an interesting statement because, at the end of the day, did Christopher Columbus actually discover America, a land that was already occupied by Indians? Or did he just come in and take up residence the same way immigrants do today? The moral of my story is to just accept differences, embrace change, learn from one another, and grow. If nothing else, you learn about others and gain a sense of understanding as to why they do what they do.

There are some key benefits that a more diverse leadership team can bring to the table, such as experience and perspective of a broader range. As a result of diversity in leadership, we can develop a greater understanding of employees, clients, and prospects. Market share is captured and maintained through innovation, which requires experience, perspective, and relatability.

Also, positive change is more likely. The top leadership group is more likely to agree with the decisions made by executives with diverse backgrounds, whereas executives without diversity make fewer positive changes and make decisions that aren't agreed upon. There is also a greater awareness of the issues. As we live our lives, we are able to filter everything and everyone around us through a powerful filter. You become more aware of the landscape your organization must navigate when you increase the diversity of filters on your leadership team: employee needs, customer experiences, social impacts, and global opportunities. It also enhances opportunities for growth.

By bringing diverse perspectives to the leadership team, assumptions and judgments can be pressure-tested. As a result, a learning organization that is open to testing and new ideas will uncover new ways of thinking, encourage a growth mindset, and promote a growth mindset in the workplace. As a result, employees become more engaged, empowered, and decision-making becomes faster. It brings more valuable perspectives as well. Diversity can be a success or a disaster, depending on how culturally intelligent and inclusive the team is. They can make better decisions when they are able to see a situation from a variety of angles, provided that all voices have the opportunity to be heard.

There is also a stronger collective outlook. By having a diverse leadership team, the organization and its culture are shaped by a wider range of lived experiences and backgrounds. A collective outlook can be created by bringing together different perspectives and helping to spot blind spots at an early stage. Across different levels of the organization, it weaves richness in understanding, insights, and engagement. There is also more innovation. Organizations can boost innovation, attract top talent, and appeal to clients who focus on inclusion by assembling a cohesive, diverse leadership team. Leadership teams that deliver real benefits require discipline, listening, and the courage to thrive and be diverse and well-managed.

Not only is diversification dependent on religion, nationality, color, etc., but it also comes from everyone's different upbringing and experience. For example, I used to work in a corporate environment that was very structured and strict. There was a lot of turnover of employees. Eventually, we had a new office manager who came from a very different background. He set up a break room, which was simply a room with a mini play golf area, music, and so on. This room was meant as a de-stressing room. When people felt pressured or stressed and needed a break, they could go in there and let off some steam with golf or music. He allowed casual Fridays where employees could wear casual clothes on Fridays. He had events, like Friday night movie nights, where everyone would gather and enjoy a night at the movies or even a movie rental, where we all watched it in the conference room but got to let our hair down and relax with each other. It was a totally new and different approach to how things were ever done in this business, but having an open mind and trying new ideas brought in by someone from a different background made a huge difference. Employee turnover was almost non-existent after that.

Diverse training can encourage employees to value others' opinions and accept differences. Diversity initiatives in the workplace can be strengthened and cultivated through awareness training. Open-mindedness is important for any business type. Nowadays, with different races, genders, etc., this can create a more solid acceptance.

Employee retention and turnover costs can be reduced by diversity, including diversity of gender, religion, and ethnicity. When employees feel respected and valued for their unique contributions, they are more likely to remain loyal. An open-minded, global company culture can be fostered by promoting inclusiveness and diversity at work. As well as making your workplace more interesting and enriching for everyone, this will help your company better understand colleagues, clients, and customers around the world. The world has finally started to recognize the importance of this fact and actually started to embrace it.

Stay informed about global events and international politics, as well as different cultural traditions and approaches to work. Discover the differences between your colleagues from different countries. Travel opportunities should not be ignored, especially if you have the opportunity to visit overseas offices or teams. Besides gaining a deeper understanding of culture and sensitivity, you're likely to find much in common with your new friends as well. Take an active role in seeking out new perspectives and ideas.

Are you having trouble solving a problem at work? Make use of new perspectives by asking for help. The way people approach business issues may differ based on their culture or background. Despite their differing life experiences, your colleagues will be able to offer you valuable insight. By seeing something from a different perspective, a solution is often revealed that you wouldn't have considered otherwise.

Different perspectives can foster productive business relationships when they are valued and embraced at work. A company culture that fosters a sense of inclusion and better communication will flourish whether you are in a junior role, a manager, or a director. By fostering an inclusive work environment, your company will be able to retain diverse talent and attract global talent.

Most importantly, you should make sure others are treated in the same way you would like to be treated. That is the #1 rule. No one is better than the other. Different, yes, but better or worse? No. Everyone needs to be treated equally.

In a diverse professional environment, you shouldn't always follow the so-called Golden Rule. The Platinum Rule, which is based on treating people how they would like to be treated, is the better course of action.

Consider and respect the boundaries and expectations of others at all times. Someone else in your company may have values that conflict with yours. Taking cultural nuances into account can even be commonplace in day-to-day interactions. You can avoid misunderstandings by understanding how different cultures perceive handshakes, eye contact, and personal space boundaries.

Don't hesitate to ask questions when in doubt. Don't be afraid to apologize if you accidentally offend someone. You will be appreciated by your colleagues for your sensitivity and effort in both scenarios. Your workplace will be more welcoming and productive if you respect personal and cultural boundaries and encourage your colleagues to do the same. Ironically, many people understand the lack of understanding and won't hold you responsible for perhaps shaking a hand wrong (in their culture) or a simple salutation done incorrectly. They do, however, greatly value you asking questions to learn and understand, as it proves you are interested in their culture and want to learn more about them.

It's important to also learn about the traditions, celebrations, and holidays of other cultures. There are many online calendars that highlight many cultural and diverse backgrounds and situations, so why not highlight them at the office? It would make your staff feel noticed and appreciated. They have Black/African American holidays, Hispanic/Latino American holidays, holidays for women, holidays for persons with disabilities, Islamic holidays, etc. Learn about them and share them with your staff.

A culturally diverse holiday calendar can be one of the easiest and most fun diversity and inclusion activities. Find appropriate ways to celebrate different traditions with your colleagues. You need to ensure your workplace is culturally diverse as it brings life to your business.

Here are some celebrations of diversity:

April is Celebrate Diversity Month. It was started in 2004 to recognize and honor the diversity surrounding us all. By celebrating differences and similarities during this month, organizers hope people will gain a deeper understanding of each other.

May 21 is World Day for Cultural Diversity for Dialogue and Development; a day set aside by the United Nations in 2001 as an opportunity to deepen our understanding of the values of cultural diversity and to learn to live together better.

October brings Global Diversity Awareness Month to remind us of the positive impact a diverse workforce of men and women can have on society.

The first full week of October marks National Diversity Week, founded in 1998 to raise awareness about the diversity which has shaped and continues to shape the United States. It's celebrated on a city or company-wide scale across the US, though some organizations observe it at other times of the year.

The third Monday in October is Multicultural Diversity Day, a national day created by Cleorah Scruggs, a fourth-grade teacher in Flint, Michigan. This day was adopted as a national event by the NEA's 1993 Representative Assembly to "increase awareness of the tremendous need to celebrate our diversity collectively."

There are many forms of diversity. Your cultural contribution to the workplace should not be underestimated. Your unique perspective, culture, and experiences can enrich others' professional experiences, no matter what your background is.

Make a positive contribution to your company's culture by setting an example. You can start a conversation by sharing a treat from home or inspire others to do the same. Looking at a calendar of holidays from around the world, why not share a treat with your staff from each culture once a month? Doing a simple online search will show you various holidays from around the world. If you have staff from other countries, how great would it be if you asked them to share a treat with everyone from their country once a year? My grandmother used to make Polish Kołaczki, which is a Polish filled cookie/pastry. Sharing these with fellow employees and sharing a bit of my family's culture would be very heartwarming. (Not to mention, these pastries are delicious!)

Diversity can be promoted in the workplace by building an understanding of diversity. Inclusion and welcoming work environments are enhanced when you know your colleagues personally, develop an appreciation for their differences and cultivate common ground.

Diverse workplaces achieve competitive advantage not just by acknowledging diversity but by creating an inclusive environment where employees can work together toward a common objective while feeling supported, thus increasing productivity and commitment.

Diversity is essential to staying relevant and thriving in an ever-changing marketplace. Your brand can be strengthened if your workforce is diverse. Additionally, you will be able to attract highly talented employees and achieve lower turnover.

Enhance your leadership skills by being inclusive. Get the conversation started. Make sure everyone is treated with respect. Transparency and accountability should be increased. Assist in the advocacy process. When discussing and making decisions, notice the diversity. Change begins with reflection and commitment.

The most important scenarios for leveraging diversity are:

- Making a difficult decision or solving a complex problem.

- Using diversity to your advantage:

- Ensuring that the room is suitable

- Making sure you don't speak first

- Being objective when listening

- The quiet ones need to be attracted

- Being willing to change

- Ensuring robust debate takes place

The world is seen differently by every culture, every nationality, and every individual. In a similar fashion, every culture, nationality, and person has a different perspective, knowledge, and point of view. Bringing together all of these different viewpoints can produce miraculous results.

Bringing people together and evolving and growing and sharing and changing and evolving even more is what brings forth change and growth. We may not always agree with everything, but taking a little here and there and incorporating things for further growth is fundamental to the bigger picture. Change is good, and diversification allows us to change in ways we may not have ever considered prior. It also educates everyone, and growth continues even further.

The world is full of wonder and potential and bringing diversification together in the workplace brings the same possibilities to you. Embrace it. Learn from it. Grow from it. Flourish with it.

ABOUT THE AUTHOR

Patricia Baronowski-Schneider in an IR/PR/marketing expert who works in driving brand awareness for her clients through integrated marketing.She is a two-time bestselling author with over thirty years of experience working with all types of niches around the world.

Leveraging a Diverse Workforce

Ira Bowman

D iversity means different things in business, whether on a team or in the entire organization. It's not simply about their nationality or education level, but more about the person's competence at being able to do the job while not disregarding any professional requirements. I wouldn't want a doctor to operate on me if they weren't qualified. Diversity with respect to the minimum standard or minimum qualifications to do a specific type of work, but outside of that, throw away any preconceived notions that you have in hiring or building a team.

Ageism is a big one these days, as is English as a first language. It could also be with respect to religion or political beliefs. If you're liberal or if you're conservative, you may not feel comfortable working with the other side of the aisle. However, a diversity of ideas can often strengthen the whole. To me, diversity is getting beyond your comfort zone and working with a team that may not look or think like you but have ideas that are just as important and can contribute to the objective—being the best at whatever you do.

Diversity in the workplace is important because it helps get to the best ideas fastest, avoiding trial and error. It helps to bring in a multitude of experiences. If everybody is cut from the exact same cloth and has the exact same experiences, it's unbalanced. We need diversity of ideas, experience, and wisdom.

Education and experience—those are the things that help to prevent mistakes and get to the best results faster. It also helps to show equal opportunity fairness. When you look across an organization and see a diverse team with a great culture, the organization is probably not cherry-picking certain types of people based on ethnicity, age, or experience. Diversity is my answer to making fewer mistakes and getting faster results.

Diversity as a leader is important. Going back to the idea of getting to the best solutions faster, I have a certain set of experiences, education, and knowledge. Having a diverse team allows me to draw from the experience and wisdom of others. There may be pitfalls out there that I can avoid simply by listening to the diverse team I hire that has a variety of experience and education. Where they live, what schools they went to, what subjects they studied, their geopolitical affiliations—it all makes a difference when it comes to the strength of the circle. The bigger the circle, the more competent the circle is, the better a leader will be, and the better position they'll be in.

It also indicates a certain mentality that says, *I don't have to be the only smart person in the room. I don't need only those people who think like me.* When creating an organization that's healthy, it comes down to culture. Having a leader who is open to a diverse team signifies that they are not only self-secure, but they are open to answers coming from outside of their main influence, belief system, experience, and logic set. With a diverse team, you increase the size of the skill set. You can draw out the answers and minimize and mitigate risk by including a more diverse team.

Diversity is important as a leader for all of those reasons and also because it sets a good example. You may not need a lot of help in a specific field, but your team says a lot about you and can help with your legacy.

I don't think there's a situation where a diverse team would be negative. In every case I can think of, a diverse team is better for solving issues when you have different races, nationalities, political affiliations, and even socio-economical differences. Those variances help to increase or broaden the experience of the collective group. The information and experience subset grows, which gives the team the ability to draw from a wider set of knowledge to avoid and resolve problems faster, and to come up with something that is fairer and avoids pitfalls. Likely, a narrower subset wouldn't have considered the overall solution.

What problems in the workplace can be solved through diversity? Sometimes it's better to have one person for speed—maybe they're just really good at their thing. But when you have a group environment, you need a group—with the exception of a minimum qualification to be a part of it. For example, they may need to be doctors, lawyers, or engineers, but once that minimum education requirement is met, diversity can come into play. Whether it be age, race, religion, or political affiliation—diversity can be beneficial to the overall formulation and composition of the solutions for whatever problem you may face, from HR to administration to production to sales to marketing across the board. Diversity can help with external communication and also resolving problems internally.

Promoting diversity in the workplace mainly falls on the owner, the ownership team, and the human resources department, but there's marketing involved in it too. How can we better promote diversity in the workplace? If we have a responsibility outside of our organizations to promote diversity, then it starts with our dollars and how we spend them. If you want to promote something and encourage others to do more of that, then you use your dollars to vote. It's the language everybody seems to understand and listen to.

Spend your money with vendors, corporations, or organizations that align with your diversity preferences. If you want to promote better diversity in an organization, then spend your dollars with those who have what you're looking for. If you're not able to spend your dollars with them, then you can do things like promote them on social media. You can give them a good Google rating. Refer others to businesses you think are championing or doing a good job.

Promotion, for the most part, is going to be from outside the organization. You have to make sure you are diverse and make sure your hiring practices are helping you to look the way you want to. It includes diversity. Diversity inside an organization starts with blind hiring. The ATS (applicant tracking software) was put in place to help with this by eliminating race, religion, and origin by taking the names out, thus helping to have a blind sample. In our hiring practices, we need to make it clear that we're not going to look at the applicants' age, race, religion, where they come from, or their economic standing. That will help with diversity in the workplace.

Diversity can help promote competitiveness for any business in a variety of ways. With a diverse team, you get answers faster, you bet better answers, and you avoid many pitfalls that you could have hit if you didn't have a diverse team. You have a wider base of experience and knowledge. Having a better product coming to market faster, and having fewer mistakes right out of the gate, helps you be competitive because you make a good first impression. If your team is inclusive, the more people from the outside will look in and say, "I relate." If you are hiring without consideration of race or gender or any other labels, you're just hiring the best candidates.

Many of the best people are looking for a company they can identify with. You probably won't be boycotted by any group because you aren't hiring them or purposely weeding them out. Your company, if it's healthy, should mimic the percentage of the population at large. If your company matches the population at large, you're probably not going to get targeted by any groups, which will help you to be competitive. If you match the population at large, those groups can say, "Hey, this is a company that doesn't discriminate against us." And that can be really helpful in getting that particular portion of the population to purchase your products or services.

Anti-diverse companies can have a problem internally with a lack of varied ideas and a narrow base of experience and knowledge, so they run into problems. Maybe it takes them longer to get a product to the public. They don't have the experience they need, and they've had to do some trial and error where a more diverse team would have helped them get there faster. And externally, with sales marketing itself, a diverse organization will be embraced more wholeheartedly across the board by all the subgroups out there. You'll earn more of their business than if they think you don't hire anybody who looks or acts like them. Diversity can help any business to be more competitive in those ways.

An organization can best embrace diversity by making it clear that it won't accept any form of prejudice. People don't have to agree, but respect is important. Obviously, when you have a diverse set of ideas or experiences or a variety of cultures where people are from, then you can have issues. But embracing diversity encourages rapport-building within the organization. Team-building activities and opportunities to socialize together in ways that aren't necessarily related to work will help productivity. These activities can be anything from Top Golf or trust-building. You might bring in coaches or inspirational speakers, or you might encourage people to go to a company picnic or outing. Those types of activities will help.

If you want to embrace diversity, you have to make it clear in your hiring practices that you won't discriminate in any way. And training has to include some type of cultural sensitivity, making that the groundwork of the company, including respect across the board. Don't tolerate disrespect just because people have different ideas or come from a different geopolitical background.

An organization can best leverage a diverse workforce in a variety of ways. Internally, the first thing is to be open to suggestions, whether you have an idea box or an open-door policy. Embracing and leveraging a diverse workforce to its fullest must include being open to ideas. To avoid pitfalls and maximize the talent and knowledge base that's in your organization, you need some mechanism developed and in place to be open to communication and ideas from the team—whether they be anonymous or not.

Another part of leveraging a diverse workforce is marketing. Let the world know about your diversity, maybe with social media posts featuring your diverse staff and highlighting them as part of your Employee of the Month program. Having a variety of social media and website content spotlights your diverse group and helps boost sales. By showing the world that you're diverse, you help build an affinity with the different groups that the individuals inside the organization represent.

Externally, social media and websites help draw positive attention to the different groups represented in your organization. Internal leverage is mainly about ideas. To me, that is the best part of having a diverse group—the experience they represent. Externally, I think the best thing you can do is to help shine a light on diversity. Not only is that a good example, but it helps your bottom line. You can drive more sales, generating more revenue and profit, which is often the goal of most organizations, unless it's a nonprofit, and then you can leverage a diverse workforce by showing it off.

I think people aspire to be diverse in theory, but in reality, it's uncomfortable because now you're talking about participating on a regular basis with people who think differently than you. They have different experiences, political beliefs, or religious beliefs. It can be uncomfortable, but it's worth the effort, and it's the right thing to do. We shouldn't judge people by anything other than their ability to do a task in an organization. As a business owner, I'm hiring employees because of their ability to do whatever it is I need them to do. That's all that should matter. If they're qualified and capable, they should be considered.

Growth happens outside the comfort zone, so being uncomfortable isn't necessarily a problem—it's an opportunity for growth. Not only can you become a better person by dealing with what is uncomfortable, but your organization can also grow and become better by adjusting to this new uncomfortable area. And it will get easier for your business to assimilate new talent from different sectors. It will make you better personally, but it will also make you a better organization—an example for others to aspire to.

At my company, we don't consider race, religion, sexuality, nationality, or if English is their second language—because it's the right thing to do. It might be uncomfortable at first, but it will get easier the more you practice. I encourage people to work on diversity. Make it a true goal. Make an action plan and follow through. It's worth the effort.

ABOUT THE AUTHOR

Professionally Ira is a marketing and sales expert, photographer, graphics designer, website builder, philanthropy owner, search engine optimization content writer, and TEDx speaker. Ira has built a large social media following with six-figure following counts on both LinkedIn and Instagram.

Ensure Success with Diversity

Dr. Julie Ducharme

Diversity is a word that is thrown around a lot today. Do we truly understand what diversity means or how subjective the word diversity is or the true role it plays in business today?

I am a woman who has fought her way to the top in a very male-dominated industry. In fact, for most of my career, I was the only woman in these big leadership positions. Diversity was staring me in the face daily. I regularly sat in on the cigar and whiskey time with my male colleagues as the only woman; I didn't drink or smoke, but I had to fit in, so that's where you would find me.

Diversity and its meaning have become more complicated over the years. Today, when we look at diversity in the workplace, the list has changed to include the following:

- Language

- Culture

- Religion

- Sexual Orientation

- Skills and Abilities

- Education and Background

One area of diversity that comes to mind is the diversity of men and women. As I have grown in my industry, I have come to realize that diversity encompasses so much more than just men and women and different cultures. Some of the best organizations are top in their industry because they have diversity of thought, they have people with diverse skills, and they allow their company to be innovative and, in turn, create diversity in many aspects of their business. To run a successful company, you must see diversity for all it is, not just a one-sided view, but a 360° view of what diversity can do for your company.

Twenty-three years ago, I started my first company. It was and is today a company that focuses on events and fun characters like superheroes, princesses, and mascots that show up at your events. I decided I wanted to take my company up a notch and start bringing in people like stilt walkers, fire dancers, and amazing hula hoopers. But where do you find those people? Well, that would be the circus.

Now let's put this into perspective. I was raised in rural America in a conservative farming family. This business I was running was nothing I had ever experienced growing up. We had birthday cake for parties and had family over, and that was it. But in a major metropolitan city, people pay thousands of dollars to create elaborate events for their kids, so having circus people at their event was a win. But I had never dealt with circus people before. If you have ever met someone who travels with a circus, they're quite different from what you run into daily, but these people can do amazing feats. I quickly realized that, as strange and foreign as their behavior and lifestyle were to me, I needed their talents and diversity in my company, and I had to put aside my upbringing, which was screaming at me not to work with them.

I share this story because I want to be very honest and give a transparent look at how leaders often struggle when they bring something diverse into the company that is far from what they are comfortable with. I soon learned that these very talented but different people I was hiring were fantastic people. Sure, they looked and acted differently from what I was used to, but their skills were unparallel to what anyone else could do. With a little training, we learned to work together well and soon took my company to another level. Having these people, who most companies did not have or were not willing to find, made my company desirable for people to call and book. Although my situation of searching for circus people to be part of my company might seem unique, how often do we struggle as leaders to bring in something or someone very different, diverse, and innovative because of fear? Do we fear dealing with the discomfort of change? My motto is, *If you want your company to be diverse, get comfortable being uncomfortable.*

When we take a 360° view of diversity, there are several components that exist besides cultural and gender differences. There is also diversity of thought, diversity of innovation, diversity of skills, and diversity of people. Although that diversity can include people with physical limitations, having physical limitations does not mean they are not intelligent or can't contribute.

I often even hear this about hiring veterans. People worry that they'll have PTSD and might behave strangely, but our veterans are some of the top-trained people in the world. Yet, being different keeps us from hiring them. It is important for leaders to recognize the types of workplace diversity. When diversity is present in all areas, we can see increased productivity, increased creativity, improved cultural awareness, a positive reputation created, and even an increased marketing opportunity.

Diversity improves the workplace by allowing employees to have a sense of belonging. When employees feel like they belong, it increases productivity and creates a positive culture. Diversity of thought brings in a culture that allows people with different thoughts and ideas to contribute to projects. And let's add that this also brings in people who are not just creative but also those who may be more logical or analytical as well.

However, just because you have diversity of thought in the organization, it does not make everyone feel like they belong. It could work against you if every single person has a far different view, which is why you must find a good balance of diversity of thought. Your people still need to keep the mission and vision of the company at the forefront of their goals.

Many leaders are pairing people together who have two highly different backgrounds and skills sets, which at first can seem like a bad idea as these two people try to see how each other works, but in the end, they will end up balancing each other out and provide a well-rounded, diverse thought process. I think the most important thing is that by achieving workplace diversity, you will bring out the best in your employees. And this will allow them to find and reach their full potential.

When a leader integrates diversity into their leadership and organization, it brings a greater perspective and depth to the organization. It creates the ability for leaders to find relatability in their clients as well as their employees. Understanding all aspects of diversity of a leader is crucial to organizational success.

As a leader of several organizations, I want my perspective to be challenged. I want openness and passion for diversity of thought in my organizations. I want my teams to know their thoughts are important in the work we do and that I value them. As a leader, I want my thoughts challenged to know I am as innovative as I can be.

When I can increase the diversity of leadership in my organization, I will increase awareness as well. What do I mean by this? Well, we all have been shaped by our experiences, and those experiences make us more aware of different situations and how we handle them. As you diversify your leadership, you diversify your ability to have awareness in a variety of areas and bring in a competitive advantage.

Another aspect to consider is bringing new ways of thinking to the organization. I remember having a lovely student assistant from a very remote part of the world. I loved working with her. She would fill me in on how she grew up, why she thought the way she did, and how her culture handled situations. It was enlightening and refreshing and helped give me a perspective on how international students may feel and why it was important they were part of our organization. She brought in a new way of thinking and new opportunities that I may not have ever considered.

I tell my kids constantly we must get out of our "American Bubble" and see what the world has to offer; our way is not always the best way. When we, as leaders, embrace the differences in thinking, skills, and culture, we can create better employee engagement.

A versatile leadership group also helps with fast decision-making. In the current business world, things are constantly changing, and a more diverse leadership team can bring in a diverse perspective full of rich experiences that can help make decisions faster and more efficiently. How often, as leaders, have we said, "I am not sure this has ever happened to me before"? How great would it be to have many diverse leaders from many industries and from different parts of the world who could say, "I have dealt with this successfully, and this is what we need to do."

Another way to think about this is that diversity helps bring in top talent. When our job postings are closed-minded, they tend to bring in close-minded people who think how we think. Even how we interview people could turn them away from the job. When I talk about our very innovative initiatives, it draws people with exceptional talent to us because they want to be part of a company that is so innovative. Companies like Google and Zappos, who are employee-first companies, find people will stay longer with them because they feel appreciated, accepted, and part of something bigger.

Have you ever entered a store and you can feel how miserable the workers are and how their unhappiness rubs off into how they deal with the customer? When we have diversity in our organizations and leadership, we can work on building better relationships with our customers and employees. Then our employees feel accepted and part of the company. They become more engaged, and they serve the customers of the company in a more positive way.

I have mentioned this before, but diversity in leadership brings in more innovation. When you work with people who have worked all over the world, the different perspectives are nothing short of amazing. To have advice from each leader who has dealt with different cultures, countries, and processes is a win-win for everyone. It's like suddenly you have this giant library of information at your fingertips because your people have seen it all, heard it all, and been part of the experience. After all, that's the secret behind better productivity, creativity, and improved employee engagement.

When I think about companies that have embraced the 360 version of diversity, it starts with creating the right diverse culture. I feel no one has done this better than Zappos. I had the opportunity to not only tour Zappos but also have an event at their corporate offices and do training with their people. I got to see their ball pit and jump in it, check out their gourmet coffee stations, and go to their bowling alley. I also saw how everyone was working together—no offices, no cubicles. It was very open, which included the CEO, who was right there in the middle of all of them working.

I was shocked a bit at first. I thought to myself, *How can anyone get any work done with all these fun distractions?* Mind you; my work started in cubicles and lots of offices and top-down leadership. It's only been in the last ten years I have seen the transformation and flat-line leadership approach. But the more I toured, the more I saw this phenomenal culture that was so different, but employee centered. I had never seen an organization so focused on the happiness of its employees and diversity. As I dove into questions with my tour guide, they highlighted some important things about their culture. They treat everyone like family—customers and employees. They believe leaders must show in their actions that everyone, whether it be customers or employees, must have a 5-star experience with Zappos.

Next was the hiring process, which was so intriguing to me. Everyone I met in Zappos had an outgoing and friendly personality. I often find it rare in large organizations to find every person you meet to have such a chipper attitude. It was as if I was talking to baristas at Starbucks, who always seemed extra caffeinated. I was told the company hires for "cultural fit." *What a concept*, I thought.

When Zappos hires someone, they work in all the departments of Zappos for the first couple of weeks. Then after that, they offer them 1000 dollars to walk away or not take the money and keep working at Zappos. The ones who really get it, who really fit in the culture, don't take the money; they stay. Zappos said they are looking for people who want to have fun and be passionate, as these characteristics fit with Zappos' brand and culture.

Another important aspect of Zappos is that all information is shared with everyone, meaning from profits to sales and more. I think what was amazing during this tour was that there was so much trust demonstrated. Zappos made 2 billion in revenue last year in 2021, and I truly think this is because of their unique culture, personality, and customer service, which all come back to trusting their employees.

I have read many articles on Tony Hsieh, and when asked what he is selling at Zappos, he states, "happiness." What a concept! For a CEO to be people-centered and more focused on diversity and inclusion of his people than the products, and with that approach, he could still create a billion-dollar company by selling happiness. It's nothing short of brilliant.

We can all take notes from Zappos on how to integrate this type of culture into our workplace. Now, let's be honest, Tony, the CEO, was brilliant and able to do this in a certain way. We can't all be Zappos with bowling allies and ball pits. But can you attempt to learn how to integrate a culture of diversity that is people-focused, hiring people to fit the culture versus the product? Yes, we can.

My takeaway from my experience with Zappos and their company culture is that they hired to fit the culture, not the product, they entrusted their employees with the most sensitive information, they treated everyone like family, like they mattered, and they believed the path to success was having fun and selling happiness. That is your recipe for creating successful diversity of thought and culture.

Innovation has been one of the biggest issues plaguing organizations. In this ever-changing business world, companies must stay innovative. If they don't, they lose their competitive edge. Just look at the computer and phone industry. Computer tech and phone tech change every six months when something new comes out. Every company is trying to find and create the next best technology to gain an edge over their competitors and get everyone to switch over to their tech. In fact, a company that has gained an edge on how to create diversity in its organization and get the most out of innovation is Google.

In the past, it's often been said that diversity is tough to measure, and people argue if it truly contributes to the success of a company. New research is showing evidence that the diversity of an organization is leading to innovation and even driving the market growth. In fact, diversity has been shown to unlock the innovation issues of corporations. When people from all cultures, skills, and knowledge come together, it allows employees to create compelling ideas that can change the company positively.

When we look at diversity, I would say that inherent diversity is only part of the equation for solving issues with diversity in the organization. Head leaders of the organization also must find what I call acquired diversity, like what we talked about with Zappos. This acquired diversity can establish the culture, which allows employees to feel like they can contribute their ideas in a nonjudgmental environment, encouraging that intrapreneurship style. Google has integrated inherent diversity and acquired diversity to put them at the top of the market in innovation.

Google's secret to success is like Zappos in that it is employees centered. Like Zappos, Google encourages creativity; they want the intrapreneur in their company to go to town with out-of-the-box thinking. If you remember, Zappos has a very open floor plan. Google takes it one step further; they do not put any rules or restrictions on where the employee must work. They want employees to create a fun workspace for themselves. And when they say anywhere, I mean anywhere—you can sit on the floor, in the lounge, and even in the cafeteria.

Another important aspect of Google's secret sauce to success in diversity is they are very transparent, like Zappos. They also have a very flat leadership level, not keeping the lower-level Google employees from sharing ideas with the upper-level Google leaders. And Google's culture encourages its employees to share and voice their opinions; they do not want quiet people. But it does not stop there. Google also offers many more amenities to make sure their employees are carefree at work to focus on work. They offer financial advisors on site, a cafeteria, and $12,000 a year in tuition support. They offer paid parental leave, with fathers getting up to six weeks off and mothers getting 18 weeks off, all paid. They allow employees to have a hybrid work-from-home or from-the-office. The lunches are free at Google, along with various cafes, restaurants, and well-stocked micro kitchens that give free meals. There are fitness facilities on site, laundromats on site, hairdressers, and even massages.

It sounds like a dream, doesn't it? Who wouldn't want to work for Google when they provide so many amenities, and why are they always on top in innovation? They also give their employees 20 percent of their time at work to work on their own projects. This often leads to innovation, and then Google will offer to buy them out or partner with them. Thus, creating a win, win, win. This is nothing short of brilliant.

When you bring in people of all skill sets, and you don't limit them in creativity, you create the most positive culture. And then, when you say have fun and play, your innovation becomes unlimited, and you solve the company's problems in leaps and bounds. Positive things happen when people have the freedom to self-express and be creative, and have a voice in an organization.

The burning question is how we can be diverse, like Google and Zappos and many other companies having success with such diverse leadership, culture, and philosophy. It's not as hard as you think. If you want to give your employees the Google or Zappos experience, change the work culture and structure you may currently have. Start with revising the company's core mission, vision, and values. What do you want your company to achieve, and how will you move in that direction successfully? What changes will you need to make in your current culture and diversity to make that happen?

I have watched companies crumble over bad communication. Communication is key to any company's success. You can have diversity, but if your communication is bad, you won't last long. Having that flat leadership line where a first-month employee can communicate with senior management is key. You never know; that employee might just have a multi-million-dollar idea. Give them a chance to tell you. As I have mentioned before, when employees feel heard and wanted, creativity will flow. There will always be good and bad ideas. Not all ideas are great, but sometimes, a bad idea can be morphed into a good idea with some brainstorming and teamwork.

Making sure you have not only top talent but also the right talent is important, and keeping that talent is vital as well. As a small business owner, it's tough to compete with places like Zappos or Google, so I don't try. My company has a small family feel, with lots of flexibility and transformational servant leadership. Some people love that feeling and love being part of something small that is making a big impact, and that is where I search for my people. We may not be a Fortune 500 company, but we will still make an impact.

If you can, I always say hire within. If you see an employee showing interest in another department or the ability to move into a leadership position, give them that opportunity. You will see more loyalty and less turnover if you invest in your people.

One of the best things I did for all my companies was not to micro-manage and leave room to be flexible. I always say I am an adaptive leader, meaning I can adapt to the situation at hand. I give my employees more flexibility, especially my tech people. I tell them as long as they make meetings and deadlines, I don't care if they work at night or day as long as the work gets done. Also, since many are independent contractors, I allow them to take on other side gigs as long as they don't conflict with what we are doing. I tell them I want them to make their maximum potential in profit, so I will not hold them back. If they can handle the workload, I am fine with it.

I think Simon Sinek put it best when he said that leaders should eat last. Servant leadership is needed to bring diversity to your company. As you can see over and over from the examples of giant companies like Google and Zappos to smaller companies like mine, you can't diversify if you don't care for your employees. Getting the best out of your employees is much more than giving them a good salary. They want to be happy at the job. They spend more time at work than they do with their family; they want to love what they do. They want to love the people they work with, and they want to have a purpose that they are making a difference. If you want to create a successful diverse culture and company, it starts with being employee centered.

Diversity has drastically changed in definition and design over the last 30 years, just like business has. To create and sustain diversity, you must be an adaptive leader. You must be able to adapt to the ever-changing business environment.

As a leader of an organization, don't lose sight of the mission and vision of your organization. Being adaptive is great, but too much adaptation could take the company in the wrong direction. It comes down to a delicate balance of creating and implementing a 360 view of diversity in your organization but staying true to your mission, vision, and values.

Leaders who want to make a change and bring in diverse thoughts, skills, and people must be comfortable being uncomfortable. Change is never easy; it never comes easy and will have moments of triumph and moments of despair. Good leaders fight through those tough moments to make it to the great moments. We are learning from Apple, Google, Zappos, and many more leaders who built incredible, diverse organizations because they were willing to be uncomfortable, go against the cultural norm, and create and foster a diverse culture. I challenge you to dig deep and find the right path of diversity for your organization.

ABOUT THE AUTHOR

Dr. Julie Ducharme is a sought-after keynote speaker, author, business consultant, entrepreneur, instructor, and special consultant in women's empowerment. She is the creator, founder, and CEO of Julie's Party People, JD Consulting, Synergy Learning, and Taylor Elite Sports.

Developing a
Diversity Mindset

Lynn Hoerauf

A quick response to the question, "what does diversity mean" is "everyone is not the same as everyone else." Yet, diversity is so much more than that. It is a fabric that provides rich textures, color, and vibrancy to our lives and workplace.

Yes, we are different from each other, gloriously, marvelously, intriguingly—and even amusingly—different from each other. We have unique perspectives and ways of thinking and relating to the world. We have distinct backgrounds and experiences, and even our brains work differently. Our eyes see through varied lenses, and our minds gather and process information in our own ways. These differences determine whom we marry or if we decide not to marry. They provide a framework for which education or careers to pursue. It affects the way we manage money and raise our kids. In many ways, our differences make the world go round.

These variations can be exciting and sometimes unsettling to us. It can be challenging when interacting with someone who looks at the same thing we see but interprets it entirely differently. When working with someone different from us in background, history, or personality style, it can be a stretch to understand their perspective or anticipate their responses to life's situations. Maybe they come up with a solution that doesn't make sense to us. Yet, this is precisely what might be needed to determine, and then achieve, the best course of action.

Our tendency may be that we are drawn to others who believe and respond similarly because that is what is familiar to us. We can anticipate how they will react in new or stressful situations. Maybe they think similarly, and it is easier to understand their viewpoints. Still, it is rewarding, eye-opening, and refreshing to encounter the 'fabric' that brings more texture, color, and vibrancy to our lives.

As business owners and leaders, we don't assume that everyone experiences the world the same way we do. When embraced, diversity is a reality of life that allows us to become stronger as individuals and teams. We appreciate and even welcome our similarities and differences for their value to our projects, relationships, and world.

Consequently, intertwined with these varied backgrounds, thought patterns, cultures, etc., there are foundational approaches to diversity. Even though we may be different from each other in many aspects, there are still many ways that we are similar. We all want to be, and deserve to be, valued and accepted for who we are, not for what we do or look like or whether we have particular talents or beliefs. Acceptance, love, and respect are ideal backdrops to the fabric of diversity.

Diversity helps us to achieve the most impressive results in the workplace. With this varied input of talents, ideas, and thought processes, our diverse work group creates the best of the best. Together, our differences design, produce, and contribute at a level that we cannot achieve alone or when coming from the same attributes, perspectives, and backgrounds.

It's important to remember that a business can achieve a broader appeal by embracing diversity within its workforce. It will produce a more balanced organization with a solid foundation and a diverse customer population.

We don't know what we don't know. So, suppose we can gather diverse populations into our business. In that case, we can gain perspectives and viewpoints and even discover cultural preconceptions or language variations that we would not have understood otherwise.

For example, when on the website of the local college campus, an employee pointed out that her friends wouldn't understand what the button named "register" meant. She said that another phrase like "start here" would be more effective for people who are trying to register for classes. There is no doubt that this organization wants to help this population. Their intention is to assist people in achieving their college education and be qualified for gainful employment. But they may be missing these potential students by not using language that makes sense to those on their website who are trying to register for classes. How great it is to have someone on the team that knows how their website can be updated to reach those who want to be students at this college.

A limited mindset could say this person is not qualified in web design; therefore, their opinion should not be considered, which may even be correct in some respects. She hasn't been trained as a web designer. Maybe she isn't aware of the best practices for web design. But a broader outlook with a win-win mindset could see the value this person offers, draw from their experience, outlook, and culture, and consider what she is saying as a way to improve and meet the needs of an ever-diverse client base.

Leaders can optimize products and services more efficiently and effectively by understanding the diversity of their teams and their consumers. By understanding and utilizing these varied characteristics, styles, and perspectives, leaders will meet the needs of their companies and customers and advance their businesses.

Leadership is about position. Not your position on the organizational chart but knowing where to position yourself at any particular time. There are times when a leader needs to work side by side with the rest of the team to fill gaps and boost employee morale, but there are also times when this same leader can set themself apart in a position that allows them to see the whole picture. Leadership, whether for a team of three or a larger organization, involves creating a vision and then translating this vision into the hearts and minds of the rest of the group.

When it comes to diversity, this strategic perspective includes acknowledging past mistakes and holes in the organization. From this vantage point, you can develop strategic insights for the future. A leader must begin with a solid roadmap for diversity within their unique framework to effectively craft a compelling vision for their organization or team. This roadmap will vary depending on several factors: location (physical or virtual), history within the organization and industry, community, availability of resources, and many other factors. No one-size-fits-all diversity package will meet the needs of any individual team or organization. Someone with a well-staffed HR department will approach this process much differently than a sole proprietor.

As a leader develops in their role and builds their skillset, an understanding and appreciation of diversity are vital. More than that, however, is the courage to self-reflect and take steps into unknown or uncomfortable areas. Leading a team or an organization is like conducting a symphony. While you may be able to produce beautiful music with only a flute section, you will have a more dynamic end product if you involve various-sized stringed instruments and percussion in your team.

Many problems can be solved in the workplace through diversity, primarily through understanding and utilizing the varied strengths and perspectives that a diverse workplace provides. It depends upon the problems to be addressed, but if there is a diverse population to draw from, you can provide more solutions for the presenting opportunities. It's possible that we may not even realize the myriad of talents within our workforce.

As you may have guessed by now, I find great value in personality typology, various assessments, and a strength-based mentality. Understanding and knowing how we best work and how we are different in thinking patterns and gifts is not only helpful in solving problems and deciding courses of action but also essential and can provide a great deal of helpful information.

When someone builds a product, they have specific supplies to work with. This screw fits that hole, but another sized one will not work. What kind of supplies or equipment, so to speak, do we have in our workforce? As individuals, we have so much more to offer than a screw that fits one hole. There are many aspects and dimensions to each one of us. Learning more about these strengths allows us to take hold of them and use them to the fullest.

I think many of us haven't fully grasped the depth of our talents. Could we start there? Could we explore, discover and utilize materials like the DISC assessment or Myers-Briggs test, or the book *Strengths Finder* by Tom Rath and begin understanding our workforce in a way we haven't yet? We can solve more problems when we know what talents, strengths, and resources we are working with.

Knowledge is power. The more we understand the benefits of something, the more likely we want and use it. Providing this background knowledge of the benefits will, in effect, promote diversity. So much of it comes down to understanding and awareness. When someone catches the fire of how it helps, they will further the cause with enthusiasm.

As stated earlier, there isn't a "diversity package" that you can copy and paste into your team or organization and walk away, never to think of it again. But why would we want to do that? Being a part of diversity is experiencing the excitement and enthusiasm surrounding this topic. In some ways, this is an effort to embrace, respect, and provide opportunities for everyone. Knowing the value of each human being is an incredible movement to be a part of.

This mindset is vital to ascertain the benefits of understanding each other, honing strengths, tweaking weaknesses, accepting people for who they are, and working together. And like any belief, the more we know about it and the more we experience the benefits firsthand, the more we are apt to take hold of it and to be enthusiastic about it.

While your diversity roadmap will be unique, there are common steps that can be taken that will help you plot out your path and several resources that can give you more insight along the way. The first step is establishing a baseline of awareness of and effectiveness in creating a diverse environment. This step is essential. You don't want to jump into hiring people that look and talk differently than you and consider this your diversity plan. This would be a reactive process rather than taking the time to develop your personalized roadmap.

There may be a need to expand your awareness of diversity. There are several free resources available that can help you. You can search for online videos about diversity in general or investigate training on personality differences and how they support and supplement each other. It would be helpful to take a few assessments to help you determine your place in the DISC, MBTI, or another similar assessment. Along with this, there are excellent resources that help you evaluate your strengths and how to use them best.

As your awareness grows, you can move into the evaluation phase. This is more difficult, as it requires self-reflection and an appreciation of those different from you. This is sometimes not easy because it may require one to admit that "I can't do it all." However, we need other people to become our best selves. To be truly effective, we all need help. You need all those people with different perspectives, skill sets, and experience to make a more balanced and effective team. You know the phrase "it takes a village?" Well, it's not just about raising a child; it's also about becoming the best version of ourselves.

Once you discover your personal and team baseline and identify the missing links in your team, it's time to create your roadmap. Your diversity roadmap will be unique to your business, team make-up, and available resources. It may include determining the gaps you presently have and charting a path to eventually fill them. If you are in a position to hire, you can use this roadmap as you advertise the position and conduct interviews. If your team is already whole, you could first move into training your staff in areas that help them stretch and develop their abilities to grow into a more diverse mindset.

We will reach our goals more effectively and efficiently when we realize that we are diverse based on our various perspectives, backgrounds, personality styles, mindsets, etc., and capitalize on these strengths. This naturally leads to not only becoming more competitive but also results.

At a fundamental level, if an organization employs a more diverse workforce, it can reach more customers or clients. Today's customers expect personalized service and attention. The competition for goods and services is intense, and with the impact of social media, any negative experiences are quickly shared with a myriad of others. Therefore, businesses are forced to focus on customer care at new levels, perhaps never seen before.

A diverse workforce allows an organization to build quality customer care from the ground up. Marketing can be developed to draw individuals from a much broader background and build a potential client base far exceeding what a narrowly focused workforce could do. Products and services can be created to meet the needs of these new markets. Finally, the level of customer care can be expanded through better awareness and employee experience to meet the needs of this growing client base.

As necessary as all of these is the organization's reputation, which will inevitably be shared on numerous social media platforms. Negative press has always been challenging to overcome, but social media takes this to a new level. Likewise, a positive and empowering customer experience shared with someone's social media friends can boost your organization's reputation more than a paid advertising campaign.

Finally, as your organization's reputation grows regarding hiring diverse populations, you will become a desired destination for qualified workers. This will place you in the position of getting to choose from the best future employees rather than taking whatever you can get.

Diversity is a mindset. Our understanding and experience help us to accept and incorporate new knowledge and to gain new mindsets. I have heard from people who have attended my workshop on Problem Solving and Personality Styles that by learning about the various styles and implementing this new knowledge with those around them, they were able to advance in their businesses and improve their relationships.

One woman said she and her husband owned a business and worked together. By learning about their various personality styles, they were able to understand each other more and harness their strengths. As she told me this, she smiled big and ended with, "And it helped our marriage, too." What a great thing to experience in their business and in their personal lives! And hearing about it made me smile big, too.

Leaders also are counted on to provide the organization's flavor. Their belief can help impart the organization embracing diversity or not so much. Often it begins with the leadership and is imparted to the team. The reality is that when a new direction is implemented, not everyone will agree with it and come on board. This can put you as the leader in a difficult situation. However, while treating everyone with respect and exemplifying your positive mindset, you will indeed affect the team. Sometimes it takes some people a little longer to see. Some will accept things more quickly than others. By realizing this, you demonstrate what it means to embrace a diverse workforce as people are on differing timetables.

Focusing on the team members who willingly and passionately welcome the vision of the leadership creates momentum all its own. It will bring along those who are reluctant at first to embrace change. Using new ways and examples of defining diversity, making it real for those employed at the organization, and the leadership's mindset can help businesses embrace diversity.

Many organizations have found the benefits of tapping into training their teams in areas of diversity. This framework provides awareness that can lead to an appreciation and understanding of those different from us. The ultimate goal is to leverage this diversity by harnessing strengths, utilizing differences, and providing a well-rounded and balanced organization. This will meet the needs of a broader client base and allow the company to be more successful in the marketplace. This kind of team becomes a powerhouse.

The development of this diversity mindset can be deliberate and organized. The initiative in organizations begins as individual team members will follow a similar path to the leadership. For example, suppose the focus on diversity starts with personality temperaments and communication styles. In that case, individuals will first work through a process of self-discovery and then learn how to integrate their strengths with the rest of their team.

Diversity, simply for the sake of diversity, won't necessarily enhance an organization's effectiveness. A "just because we have to" or "because we are supposed to" mentality doesn't cut it for the long haul. However, suppose the diversity roadmap includes a way to bring about a change in mindset regarding the value of working with a diverse team. In that case, the team members can appreciate and utilize their vast array of gifts and viewpoints. They can begin to enjoy it and see the value that it provides.

There is so much to learn from and enjoy in people, whether they are more like us or very different from us. I think of my dog, Maverick. He doesn't just like people; he *loves* them. It doesn't matter who you are or what you look like; he is all in on his love for you. If he's just met you, he wants to let you know how cool you are and how much you mean. As humans, we can sometimes compare ourselves to others, and it seems almost too vulnerable to approach the world in a Maverick kind of way. Still, I'll tell you what, he looks pretty happy, not comparing himself or wondering if he's loved you too much. This total acceptance and all-in appreciation of human beings can go a long way. Maybe we could all be a little more like Maverick.

ABOUT THE AUTHOR

Lynn M. Hoerauf is a speaker and award-winning author of the Rom-Com *Miss Snickers*. She enjoys sharing humor and insight while cheering people on as they flourish in their lives, work, and relationships.For more information, tune into her Relational Effectiveness podcast on the Strategic Advisor Board channel or go to LynnSpeaks.com.

Diversity Will Take Your Organization to the Next Level

Brianna Jackson

D iversity, to me, means more than your gender, race, or those other big categories that you hear about in the media today. Diversity includes all the little things that make you *you*. Diversity can include your values, how you were raised, where you were raised, who your influencers are, and your circle of friends. All of those different things make each of us unique. Then you add to that as you grow and develop through your experiences.

Each one of us has had our challenges. Each one of us has had our successes. Each experience is nuanced and unique to us. It's those lessons and how we internalize them that help to define us, tell us who we are, and influences how we engage in the world around us. This is the core that makes each of us so unique and special.

When you enter into a new environment, bringing your own uniqueness of thought, you cultivate the benefits of diversity. You bring together all the things that you find essential and valuable and all the experiences you've had, all you've learned— you bring your perspective. Perspective is probably one of the most important things that diversity gives us. Diversity provides the opportunity to compare differences in perspective.

Diversity taps into all those elements. It is those little elements that make every one of us unique, those little connections that our brains have formed throughout our lives—our journey, experiences, education, etc.—that make us who we are as individuals. Even if you take two similar people and put them in the same environment, each will internalize their situation at different levels. You wouldn't have the word individual if we didn't have diversity. And that's what makes us so amazing as a human race that we can each be shaped a little differently. And to celebrate and be excited to learn about each other is one of the most wonderful gifts that we have in this world.

Diversity is a critical component in being successful because it nurtures creativity. Each different perspective offers a component to generate more creative ideas and solutions. It is hard, if not impossible, to have creativity if you don't have a diverse group with different perspectives. Those non-diverse settings often result in groupthink, which hinders creative idea flow. Diversity is the very core of creativity because everybody reacts and responds to things differently, and it is that nuance and tension it can create that cultivates the flow of creative ideas.

Diversity in the workplace is critical because so much of our work is about problem-solving. To have the most effective, efficient, and productive solution, you must have diversity of thought. Diversity of thought helps to ensure that you're not just coming up with the same things that already exist. When you do that, you can't beat the competition. So having diversity is critical to ensuring that you are finding those creative and unique solutions to ensure that you have a competitive edge.

If you have diversity in your organization, you're more likely to get a much broader conceptualization of the problems that you face. And this applies even if your company isn't necessarily a problem-solving company. Having different perspectives from people of diverse backgrounds and experiences in your organization allows you to explore and analyze each situation to find the gaps and seams that could hold you back from being your best selves.

Finding those gaps and closing them gives you that competitive edge, that creative thinking, those out-of-the-box solutions to whatever product or service you're providing. And if you can tap into that, you're tapping into the goldmine that is your human resources. And that is one of the most important things that a workplace should do if it wants to succeed and be profitable and grow.

When you have diversity in your workforce, and you're promoting and using that diversity, you will increase your profit margin. Several McKinsey studies talk about and link your profitability as an organization to your diversity. They even go so far as to state that a diverse organization will yield 2.3 times greater cash flow per employee than a non-diverse organization. How you capture the diversity in your teams, how they function, and whether people feel included and able to give feedback and contribute matters because all of those factors determine if you will realize the potential to increase your profits.

This is why strong leadership is so important. One essential attribute of a strong leader is the ability to inspire those around them and support their personal growth and development. A good leader doesn't need to manage his people. A good leader has people who are willing to work, ready to sacrifice, and go the extra mile because they believe in the mission, the job, and the organization. Their belief and trust in that ensures their support, and they do so because they've been inspired by the leadership around them, and they've also been supported by that leadership.

Diversity and leadership together are critical to your success. A leader must recognize and demonstrate respect for all of these differences, nuances, and unique aspects of their teams, or they could inadvertently turn people off or, even worse, cause offense. They could be trying to inspire, and instead, somebody could feel put down. Understanding the nuances that diversity plays in those roles is vital to your leadership teams.

Diversity also gives leaders a better perspective. A leader trying to inspire their team will have a much great likelihood of success if they have the diverse perspective of their team and understand their diversity—the different attributes, characteristics, and backgrounds. It better equips them to get where they need to be. Leaders can find the right inspiration and guidance to match each member of their team in a way they can internalize. For a leader, having that appreciation is vital.

On the other side of that same coin is creating diversity in yourself as a leader. This is essential because if you limit yourself to only the same experiences, and you have not gone out there and tried to expand your boundaries and pool of influencers to ensure you stay open to different things, even things you disagree with, you rob yourself of a broad sense of understanding. You must research, think critically, and gather data about all these different situations, circumstances, and issues. It's going to make you better. If you have that diversity of experience, you're going to be much more open to creating more diverse teams as well.

As a leader, if you are very closed off and you only associate and affiliate with what is familiar to you, then you will struggle because you will be focused only on a very narrow aspect and end up missing out on the goldmine of the human resources that are available to you. If you, as a leader, are not open to more things, you will close yourself off from many opportunities and even the ability to engage with your people.

Having diverse experiences and being open to diverse things around you and in your environment will make you more open to changing the norms and more approachable to people who are different from you, exposing you to even more feedback and opportunities. If you can take all that information and use it to tune into how you lead and how you work with your team, that's what is going to drive it home and make you one of the most successful leaders possible.

I love the question: What problems can you solve through diversity in the workplace? But I would completely flip it on its head with this challenge: What problems can't you solve with diversity in the workplace? And the reason I say that is that diversity is about bringing together different perspectives that can better analyze and more creatively solve any problem.

If you're trying to solve a problem and you only have a singular group with a singular perspective looking at the problem, you will not see all the different nuances and aspects of that problem. You will zone in on what you think is the right answer right away, and you will go forth and execute that right answer, which leads you to ostracize many other opportunities and options. And what better way to solve problems than with a mixed bag of interesting perspectives that allow you to not only identify the issues you may face or the circumstances you may be in but also conceptualize things from many angles, which will help you find success in the long term.

Therefore, it is vital to have diversity, but you also have to have inclusion. If you have diversity, a mixed bag of folks with mixed bags of experiences sitting around the table looking at a problem, but they don't feel included, heard, and like their voice is going to be accepted as a contribution, they will not speak up.

So, you can't have diversity without pairing the inclusion part with it and making sure that your folks are empowered and feel comfortable providing their input and feedback. When you do that, you will get the problem looked at from so many new angles that your solution to that problem is going to perform 87 percent better, according to McKinsey studies, than the solution had you only looked at it from the lens of an individual or singular viewpoint.

That was part of the reason teams were developed in the first place. The goal was to bring different perspectives together, to bring different people with different thought patterns together to help solve problems.

As more and more research is done, there is an increasing realization that what drives the productivity, efficiency, and profitability of an organization is having diversity of thought contributing to all those problem-solving sets. Without diversity, you may get the job done, but you will not get it done nearly as quickly, efficiently, or creatively as you would if you had diversity in your team. Tackling that problem and bringing the different perspectives and analyzing it from all the different angles that they think of, that's what's going to make you successful.

To promote better diversity in the workplace, you must start with respect and openness. We all talk about being respectful, but no one teaches us how to be respectful. And unfortunately, most of what we see in mainstream media is not the best example of how to interact and engage respectfully. Therefore, you must teach people how to be respectful, debate with respect, have different opinions, and still be able to appreciate the input and differences of everyone, and how to disagree politely.

It's okay to disagree. We don't all have to think the same; that's exactly counter to what we are trying to achieve. We don't all have to interpret things the same. You must promote respect and openness to encourage more people to come to the table and share. If you can't find ways to 'agree to disagree' when tapping into your diverse team, you will inhibit openness and respect and lose people's trust and willingness to contribute.

Openness ultimately attracts diversity because people will feel heard. They'll feel comfortable giving their opinions. They'll feel comfortable joining your team if they know you will be open and listen. It's one thing to say that's how you operate. You also have to prove that with the people who work for you. If you tell them you listen to them and value their input, but you never use their input or contributions, after a while, they will not believe that you're valuing their input, and they will not only stop providing it but may also look for other places to go.

So, you must tap into that openness, teaching respectful discourse, not drawing hard lines between right and wrong or good and bad, and allowing everybody the flexibility to have those discussions in the gray and talk through the goal of coming to a consensus. We will not all agree 100 percent, but what we want to do is get a majority consensus. And if you don't agree or if you feel strongly against the consensus, then we want to make sure we're taking that time to understand the perspective that you bring or understand the reasons you disagree.

And we must be respectful in that discussion. We must be respectful of other people's emotions and feelings towards the decision so that even if we can't fix it for them and completely address their concerns, we've at least taken the time to understand. We've had good and engaged dialogue, and everyone feels heard and respected and that their input was valued even if it was not part of the final solution.

Make sure people understand that there must be a decision about whatever the situation is. But if you take the time to discuss it and you show respect and openness, that will increase the implementation of your diversity. People from everywhere will want to come and be part of your team because they know that they will be treated well and their inputs will be welcomed and valued, and that's what they're looking for.

That's what everybody wants. They want to feel valued. They want to feel like they're contributing. They want to be treated well so they can go home happy in the evenings.

If you have scores of people wanting to be on your team, you are already positioned to have a competitive edge. If you're focused on respect, openness, and inclusion, diverse candidates will want to come to your organization, which means your recruiting of top talent will be much more successful because people want to come and work for you, which gives you a competitive edge via the opportunity to hire the top talent. Thus, promoting diversity will open up a golden pool of human resources to refine your teams.

In various articles on the topic from McKinsey and Company, statistics show that the top 25 percent of companies with good gender diversity are 25 percent more profitable. If the split between men and women is at least 50/50, they are 41 percent more profitable. If you focus on the top 25 companies that are ethnically diverse, you're 36 percent more profitable.

When looking at those percentages, the opportunity for profit growth is amazing. It also proves that diversity leads to being more competitive. If my company is diverse and we have an inclusive culture of talking and communicating, then we will have better decisions, which will lead to more profits, which will make us more competitive.

If you can get the top talent across all spectrums of diversity, you will beat out your competitor every time because you will have the best people, and you will make the best competitive, creative, and collaborative decisions. And you will gain the most profit compared to all the other competition. Focusing on implementing diversity and inclusion initiatives is the key to maintaining your competitive edge and growing your business.

Unfortunately, the McKinsey articles also showed that 41 percent of managers said they were too busy to implement diversity and inclusion initiatives. I think one of the biggest obstacles to embracing diversity is fear. Leaders are afraid of equal opportunity complaints. Employees are afraid that somebody else will take their job or get the promotion they want. And so, to help your organization embrace diversity, it is crucial to focus on the team-building aspects and fight the scarcity mindset. It is important to fight the fear that only so many things are available. You must focus on abundance and remind your team that working together leads to more opportunities for promotions in the future. Diversity will ultimately lead to more opportunities for growth as a business, which will lead to higher salaries and more competitive benefits.

Focusing on the rewards that diversity will bring is one crucial way that you can embrace diversity and help your organization embrace diversity. Focusing on the positive aspects of diversity and abundance can help the individuals already part of your organization if they're struggling with fears regarding diversity. It brings the teams back together and uses curiosity toward differences instead of fear.

It is essential to focus on and build curiosity. Bringing and discussing curiosity makes diversity exciting on an individual level. And when you focus on curiosity, you will be much more successful at embracing diversity.

Talking about the profits, metrics, and numbers only takes people so far. Therefore, looking at the emotion behind these is also vital. What things encourage or prevent people from getting excited or feeling supported regarding diversity? How are you focused on those things? How are you addressing the emotional aspects of fear?

Fear, one of the biggest obstacles, takes many forms—fear of the unknown, fear of what you're not going to get because somebody else may get it because they're more diverse than you. How do you show your employees that you value them? Because if you value them and consistently show that you value them, you can help fight against that fear and instead encourage them to accept others and their ideas more readily. It's not you or them. The focus is on us. The focus is on the team. What are we doing together? How are we accomplishing things? How are we each contributing to support the organization?

How you leverage a diverse workforce depends on your business and what you're doing. It may be beneficial to help your diverse workforce to identify the gaps in your business or analyze your lowest-performing elements. Empower them to problem-solve. Have them frame the problem. Have them try to identify all the unique aspects of the problem or the setback or whatever is holding the business back from continued or increased growth. Have them try to pinpoint all the aspects of the impacts that the problem may be having across the enterprise so that you can identify key focus areas. Then have them tackle each of those key focus areas and develop creative strategies to implement.

Maybe change up the diversity in the groups a little and reorganize them every so often. If you have those groups take on a key focus area for your organization, they will come up with the most interesting solutions. If you've got them working together and they feel included and valued, and like everybody's contributing, you will get the best solutions, and you may get multiple options for solutions. You will get the best layout of possibilities for solutions that can help provide your next competitive edge or your next profit margin goal, or your next product development goal. You can put them on those types of things to make sure that you are fully leveraging their capabilities.

One of the other things you can do, and it takes a bit of pride, but you can have them analyze how your organization is doing. Have them audit how you're doing and have each of the different folks with different perspectives point out different nuances so you can pinpoint specific ways to increase employee satisfaction. This will help you find different tools or metrics to help improve employee satisfaction and company culture in the future.

Overall, diverse thought processes and metrics are the keys to pushing your organization to the next level. So, if you can leverage diversity in problem-solving and analytical attributes, the implications and the application of the benefits are infinite. Those are a couple of key examples where if your organization truly values diverse feedback, you can use your teams to provide diverse feedback both internally for your improvement as an organization and externally for your improvement to your clients and customers.

Be aware, though, that you can have diversity in writing only, and you won't reap those same benefits. You can have it in the numbers, but you will not truly have it if you're not focusing on being inclusive. Everybody needs to be comfortable contributing. If they're not comfortable contributing, you're never going to realize the value, the potential energy, that being a diverse organization has. It's one thing if you have this beautiful boulder of diversity sitting on top of the hill, but you need inclusion to move that boulder down the hill, gain momentum and speed, and break through barriers to achieve greatness.

In parting, I'll reiterate that you can't have diversity unless you have inclusion. Therefore, focusing on how to keep and promote inclusion, mutual respect, and valuing the uniqueness that everybody brings to the table are the keys to unlocking the potential of your diverse workforce. When companies do this well, they're unique, and everybody wants to work for them because they know they're going to feel good in their job and their organization. Maslow's hierarchy reminds us of our basic level needs: We just want to be part of something. We just want to contribute to something. If you're able to turn that light on within your diverse workforce and make sure that key piece of inclusion is there, that's when you will find true success, maximize your profitability, and overall achieve greatness for your people and your business.

ABOUT THE AUTHOR

Brianna Jackson, founder and CEO of Sonas, is a master at developing strategic frameworks that take an organization to the next level. A mother of four boys with 20 years of leadership and management experience in the federal government, she knows how to manage resources, build and empower teams, tackle the most daunting problem sets, and realize the maximum potential and profits for any industry.

THE GOLDEN RULE
AND DIVERSITY

MIKE JACKSON

When I was growing up, my parents taught me the Golden Rule. You treat people how you want to be treated. I use the Golden Rule in my personal and professional lives equally. To me, diversity is the Golden Rule. It is important to understand that people come from different backgrounds and cultures and have different experiences and that these differences should be celebrated, respected, and embraced.

I spent the majority of my adult life in the US Army. I started my military career in the Infantry. Back then, all of us worked hard. It did not matter what race, religion, or color they were.

We all worked hard together and suffered together. Due to that fact, we were close. Those very few who did not work hard did not fit in.

In Special Operations, everyone has a job to do. It takes everyone doing their job to ensure that the mission gets accomplished, regardless of their race, religion, color, or gender. That is how I see diversity in the workplace. Everyone has a job to do, and as long as they do their job, no one has an issue with any other part of their life.

Diversity is important as a leader, as you never want anyone to not feel as if they are an integral part of the team, no matter what position they hold in the organization. If someone does not feel like they are part of the team, then they will have a harder time with their obligation to the organization, and rightly so. This can lead to a lack of motivation, commitment, and productivity and can also affect the morale and cohesion of the team.

If the workplace does not respect diversity, it will make it hard for anyone to feel comfortable working there. For a workplace to run smoothly, it needs to respect everyone's perspective. This will enhance the efficiency of the workforce. When people feel respected, valued, and included, they are more likely to be engaged and motivated and to perform at their best.

I would say the classic military saying, "lead by example," fits perfectly here. If the leader does not use diversity in the organization, then none of the employees will feel the need to do so. On the other side of that, if the leader promotes diversity, then the employees would see that and hopefully do the same. The leader can also promote diversity with their statements as well as their actions. By showing that diversity and inclusion are important to them, they can inspire and influence others to do the same.

If a business does not support diversity, then they are most likely losing out on quality employees. Promoting diversity in the workplace is a great way to open your business to some of the highest-quality employees available. A diverse workforce brings a wide range of perspectives and ideas, which can lead to more innovative solutions and better decision-making. Additionally, a diverse workforce helps to better reflect the customers and communities that a business serves.

In my opinion, the best way for an organization to promote diversity is for it to have a top-down approach. If the leader of an organization embraces and supports diversity, then it makes it easier for the entire organization to do the same. If an employee in that organization makes a statement or an action against diversity, then the leader should act swiftly and accordingly. That way, all the rest of the employees would see the ramifications of not supporting diversity. This sends a clear message that diversity and inclusion are important and acting against those principles will not be tolerated.

Again, an organization that shows its leadership supporting diversity is the best way for an organization to support diversity. For them to also not support employees that do not embrace diversity is also very helpful.

In addition, organizations should also provide training and education programs to help employees understand and appreciate the benefits of diversity and how to work effectively in a diverse team. They can also implement policies and procedures that promote diversity, such as flexible work arrangements, equal opportunities, and anti-discrimination measures.

Another important aspect of diversity and leadership is representation. It is important that the leadership team represents the diversity of the organization and its stakeholders. This can be achieved by having leaders from different backgrounds and experiences, as well as through affirmative action and diversity hiring practices. Representation not only sends a positive message to employees and stakeholders, but it also helps to ensure that diverse perspectives and experiences are represented in decision-making.

In conclusion, diversity and leadership are closely intertwined, and promoting diversity in leadership is crucial for fostering an inclusive and equitable workplace. A diverse leadership team brings a variety of perspectives and experiences to the table, which can lead to more creative and effective decision-making. Organizations can actively seek out and recruit candidates from underrepresented groups, as well as provide mentorship and development opportunities for diverse employees. By embracing and promoting diversity, leaders can create a more inclusive and effective workplace and gain a competitive edge in the marketplace.

ABOUT THE AUTHOR

Mike Jackson's experience includes developing and implementing policies and procedures, enforcing leadership standards, and assisting clients in implementing quality programs. He is also a regular facilitator and guest speaker at national and international healthcare conferences. He also consults for the Department of Defense, where he is one of the senior advisors to the Special Operations community on all things medical.

Leveraging a Diverse Workforce

Ryan Jackson

insert photo of
Ryan Jackson

When we talk about diversity, we're specifically talking about people. And as humans, and especially culturally, we like to categorize people, which isn't inherently fair. We put them in categories according to their race, religion, ethnicity, income, etc. To many people, being diverse often means that you have a variety of people from different backgrounds, ethnicities, or sexual orientations.

However, when discussing diversity, we must also consider categories outside the traditional ways we categorize people. For example, rather than only considering someone's educational level in terms of college, it is also essential to consider other intellectual capabilities and their wiring. These could include street smarts, life experience, wisdom, thought processes, and how they approach problems. These characteristics can provide another aspect of diversity outside of where someone comes from or what they look like.

Income is another area we often think about when discussing diversity. We typically think of specific categories such as low, middle, or high income because that will impact how people approach problems and think about things. Our backgrounds can undoubtedly influence how we view things. And when we're diverse, we have a wide variety of people from different backgrounds.

Another area that could come into play regarding diversity is someone's values, morals, and ethics. But we'll discuss that more later.

Diversity is vital in the workplace from two different optics. There's the optic of looking into the business from the outside, but there's also the optic of looking at the company from the inside.

In our culture, diversity is a huge issue and a significant consideration in business. Anytime an outside entity is looking at an organization, if they see an organization is not diverse, it will reflect negatively on them. A lack of diversity can lead to negative judgments. So that's more of a consideration regarding a political correctness approach.

But I think more important is the optic from the inside. Lack of diversity can lead to discomfort for employees. If people feel like outsiders, they often feel uncomfortable. This is often clearer in larger organizations. People who are similar or fit into similar categories usually migrate to each other and interact more frequently with each other. Therefore, making sure that people feel included is integral.

Another important thing about diversity in the workplace is diverse interactions provide an environment for members of that workplace to grow. Diversity exposes people to others with different viewpoints and histories or from other places. How they have approached or had to approach life may be drastically different, and how they look at things will be drastically different. And when we take the time to interact with people with different viewpoints and backgrounds than ourselves, that will allow us to grow.

When I graduated from high school and then spent 24 years in the military, my viewpoints changed. By being around a diverse group of people, I've sought opposite views of my own. And that has allowed me to shift my viewpoints. When you have a better understanding of how other people are affected by things and the way they look at things, the history that's affected them, and the way they got to that viewpoint, it can help you grow as a person.

Diversity is essential as a leader because valuing diversity can make you a better person, and it can also make you more effective and efficient in what you do as a leader. Being a leader means you inspire people to follow you, and you also encourage them and provide growth opportunities for them so they become better people, managers, and, hopefully, leaders themselves. Therefore, providing a diverse environment is a good way for leaders to help those they lead to learn, grow, and be effective and efficient in their work.

Overall, diversity benefits leaders and the groups they lead. And again, I'm not only referring to the standard categories of diversity, such as how people look, their religion, and their sexual orientation, but I'm also referring to various backgrounds, such as education, thought processes, political viewpoints, and those other things that are subcategories we rarely consider.

Another way diversity affects leadership is effective problem-solving. If you don't have a diverse group, it is easier to get stuck in a groupthink mentality. If every time you approach a problem, everybody is coming at it from the same viewpoint, the same method that they solve problems with, then eventually, you're going to find a problem that you don't solve correctly, or you solve inefficiently or ineffectively, and it's going to compound and create more issues.

Therefore, it's important to have critical thinkers, creative thinkers, and people who approach problems from different viewpoints. That way, when you present a problem brought to your team, you're looking at it from several angles, and you're not missing something because of your unconscious biases. Having a diverse group of people helps combat those unconscious biases.

I hope that if you have overt biases, you can recognize those yourself and overcome them through personal development because if you have overt biases and you're implementing those into your leadership, that can be a very negative thing. But I think the biggest key is that diversity prevents unconscious biases at the table when you're discussing things. It also provides different angles of approach towards a problem and not just how to solve the problem, but what the problem is. The way a leader interprets a problem may be different because he's looking at the macro level—he's not boots on the ground; he's above the force, looking at the force as a whole and not at the trees. The people within the trees may point out things you are unaware of as a leader. So, making sure that you surround yourself with a diverse group of people and that you are open to their suggestions and criticism is essential as a leader.

Ultimately, diversity can solve any problem. Now, I will agree that some issues are minor. For instance, if we need five pens, diversity alone won't solve that. We need to buy five pens. However, how can diversity affect that? Well, some people may like different styles of pens. They're more efficient with certain pens, even though you may not usually use them. Now we use computers for most things, but someone may have a physical impairment that requires them to use a particular pen because maybe their hand cramped up or something like that. Someone may point out, looking at it from a diverse viewpoint, from the way they approach problems and think, that instead of having black, maybe we should have blue because blue will have a more significant impact on us when we do our work. So, diversity can affect all the problems we solve, regardless of size.

However, I would say that the larger the problem, the more critical it is to consider diverse perspectives. When you get extensive, complex problem sets, you need those different viewpoints. Once again, this helps to break down the problem, evaluate what the problem is, and find the solution. Diversity also helps bring to light any secondary or tertiary effects that could be part of the solution you're implementing. In short, any problem can be solved by diversity. However, it will be more effective and more critical with larger problem sets that are more complex.

How can we promote diversity in the workplace? First, we must be intentional about bringing people with diverse per-spectives into our organizations. And once again, I'll stress that it's not necessarily the standard categories we use to measure diversity metrics. Being diverse is more than skin color and sexual orientation.

We live in a culture where self-learning is more accessible than ever. Many exceptional thinkers lack high levels of traditional education. There are plenty of people out there who are super intelligent and super smart and have sought knowledge on their own outside of the conventional organization or schooling, and they are brilliant in certain subjects compared to other people who went to a traditional school. Therefore, it is essential to consider even diversity from diverse and open-minded perspectives.

The second thing to consider when bringing people into the organization is that to truly be diverse, you must bring them in early and include them at all levels. It is important to value diversity at all levels and at all stages of business growth and development. Diversity is not a box to check. You should foster diversity from the people you bring in at the lowest levels and promote them throughout the organization as part of the organization.

If you only bring diverse people in from the traditional perspective of diversity at higher levels, others in your organization may think you're just trying to check the diversity box. And that can cause a lot of problems that are going to be counter to promoting diversity, specifically promoting an inclusive environment and supporting people who have worked hard to help the company succeed.

Therefore, the other part of this is promoting diversity within the workplace for the people who are already there. And unfortunately, I think the trend right now is that companies will hold annual trainings on diversity and talk about how important it is to be diverse. They'll discuss how important it is that people don't look like each other and people don't have the same sexual preferences or be the same gender. They focus on that, and then they go about their business. What they don't do normally is they don't provide the culture and the environment where they're regularly addressing diversity through inclusion. We must make sure that we include people because when we aren't diverse, people tend to go to their little groups that they're comfortable with that probably look and feel like they do, and that doesn't help promote diversity. It can also cause animosity within the workplace.

It's important to build a culture where there are activities and open discussions to promote inclusion. When you're holding important meetings within the organization, make sure that you are inviting people to the table who are diverse—and, once again, not necessarily diverse because they look different from you. If you have somebody at the table who looks different from you but thinks the same way, that will not help bring diverse perspectives to the organization. And then people who have a different thought process and have good inputs are sitting on the outside of the table or not even in the room, and they don't feel included. There's no benefit of having diversity if you don't have inclusion as well because then you look diverse on paper, but you're not operating as a diverse organization with a diverse and open-minded culture.

So how can promoting diversity help a business be more competitive? Once again, there are two optics for this as far as how they can be competitive. There's the outside view where if an organization is seen and known as being diverse, they are more likely to be hired to provide a product or service over other organizations that aren't as diverse in how they look and execute.

With the outside optic, people will be more likely to want to join diverse organizations. If you are indeed a diverse organization in how you look and operate, then you will attract better talent that wants to be part of your organization. Diversity, therefore, also benefits you in acquiring good talent from those demographics that aren't included in other organizations, and they're missing out.

The other thing that can make you more competitive by truly being diverse, operating diversely, and thinking diversely is that your people will be happier. And when you're happier, you will be more effective and efficient in your work. You will be more willing to focus on what you're doing and to give your all to the organization. And in the end, it will provide better results. And the same goes for all levels, whether it's the entry-level workers, the middle management, or senior management—a positive culture and happiness play throughout all those different levels to provide a better result. And when you face problems that require a diverse approach to solving and implementing the solution, you will end up with a better product or service. And that will provide customer satisfaction outside of the organization, ultimately increasing the revenue for the organization to grow and become even more successful.

I believe there are two significant ways that an organization can best embrace diversity. The first is to make sure that you are recruiting from diverse sources. If you currently have a certain model to recruit talent, evaluate it, and make sure that you are recruiting from various demographics and not just one set area. If you need workers with degrees, maybe recruit at historically black colleges or other colleges. Look for nonstandard models to gain talent. Make sure that when you're taking applications, you look at things other than the checks on the boxes that put a person into a specific category. Look at the person's skill set, education, and work experiences, and choose based on that.

Another demographic that gets discriminated against and could most likely bring in some very different viewpoints is people who have been incarcerated. Organizations often have a box you must check if you have ever been convicted of a felony. This makes it hard for people to get a job once they have served their time and paid their debt to society.

By categorizing people by the boxes they check, you can hit different metrics, at least on paper, to show that you're diversely hiring. But are you hiring diverse people when it comes to their backgrounds, education, and the way they approach problems? To do this, you must look for creative ways in your application process to identify diverse people. For example, instead of checking boxes for race, ethnicity, or sex, maybe you have boxes if they are critical or creative thinkers or creators, optimizers, or implementers. Ask those types of questions. Those things are more important to a diverse team than looking differently.

The other way that an organization can embrace diversity is through leadership. People follow the example set by those who lead them or manage them. There is a difference between a manager and a leader. A manager just manages people, whereas a leader inspires people to follow them to do things. But I think it's important that leaders and managers are trained well not only about being diverse and accepting diversity but also about being inclusive to bring all types of people into the conversation, solve problems, and get the job done. If managers and leaders know it's okay to value diverse perspectives and have the proper tools to carry themselves, the people who work for them or with them will pick up on that and follow the example.

It's difficult for someone at the bottom rung of an organization to have influence going up the organization's chain. It's much easier for the tone to be set at the top. That way, people at the bottom are comfortable practicing inclusion of diversity and not worrying about being alienated. And when the entire organization is doing it, you'll genuinely embrace diversity and have diverse workers to solve problems and provide better solutions.

The best way for an organization to leverage a diverse work-force is to ensure that you're building diverse teams within the organization. You want to ensure that you don't have people on the team who all think the same way, have the same back-ground, provide the same solutions, and look at problems the same way. Make sure you have a diverse group of people to approach different issues at all levels.

An additional point that is counterintuitive to what we've been discussing so far is that while it's important to have diversity in almost everything—whether it be race, ethnicity, religion, gender, sexual orientation, education, thought processes, or viewpoints—there's one thing that an organization cannot have diversity in, and that is the diversity of core values. Every organization should have identified core values, and every member of that organization should value those things that the organization values.

That doesn't mean that they are prioritized the same. The company's core value may not be the primary value of the individual, but the individual still needs to value what the organization values. For example, if one of the core values for your organization is servant leadership, but you have a member of the organization who either doesn't believe in it or understand it and cannot be educated and trained enough to grow to the point to value servant leadership, then that person does not fit in that organization and should not stay there.

Now, this is an original thought. I've always felt this, but I could never express it until I read Jeff Duden's book *Discernment*. In that book, he lays it out clearly. And it resonated with me that, yes, diversity is valuable in everything except one thing. You cannot have diversity in the organization's core values for the organization to succeed, grow, thrive, and meet its vision.

Black and White— or Brilliant Color?

Michael Markiewicz

L et's discuss what diversity means and how implementing it is good for organizations, businesses, and individuals. I understand diversity to mean the embracing and inclusion of people from all types of backgrounds, ethnic, national, religious, sexual orientation, and identification. Each and every individual has the ability to contribute to the larger society. Every individual can teach the rest of us something, and we can learn from him/her. Diversity also means mirroring the society around us.

Diversity is instrumental to our understanding of the larger society. No matter the background or identification, I believe that each of us knows what we know, and I also believe that we know what we don't know. In the workplace, by bringing people of diverse backgrounds and identification together into the knowledge and understanding pool, we can draw upon them to understand and learn about those things we don't know but perhaps need to know to be more productive.

Imagine the possibilities of incorporating different business practices based on one diverse group's history with the business practices of another's. You suddenly have two points of view and two possibilities for resolving problems and dealing with issues. And then, imagine bringing other diverse groups into an organization, and the possibilities are far more plentiful.

While leaders don't know everything, a great leader knows how to marshal the talents and knowledge of the people they lead so they can identify where those ideas and practices can be matched with others who may not have that same set of ideas and practices and skills.

A great leader leads, and having a diverse workforce that the leader is aware of is important in developing and enhancing the workplace for everyone. It also contributes greatly to a better understanding of the world around us. Additionally, having a diverse workforce provides opportunities for everyone to contribute.

In any society or subset of society (the workplace is a subset), there often exists prejudice and bigotry, a sense of superiority vs. inferiority. In my opinion, all of these issues are learned behaviors rather than innate ones. And as many of us have seen and witnessed, that sense of superiority vs. inferiority is destructive in its essence.

By bringing together diverse people and by having those people working together to accomplish the objectives as laid out by the leader of the organization, people can begin and progress to unlearning those destructive behaviors.

It was Oscar Hammerstein II who wrote the lyrics to *South Pacific*, which go something like this:

"You've got to be taught to hate and fear
You've got to be taught from year to year
To hate all the people your relatives hate
You've got to be carefully taught."

He wrote those lyrics in the late 1940s, and while relevant then, they are just as relevant today. By taking the ego out of the equation, we create a more inclusive and productive and knowledgeable society and workplace.

It begins with the hiring process. Reviewing resumes without regard to examining the ethnicity of the name on the resume, without regard to assuming the religion or color of a candidate, but with regard for accomplishments, history in the workplace and education goes a long way in promoting diversity, not only in the workplace but in life.

Think about how much richer our cultures and society are when we can learn from and sometimes adapt knowledge and practices to our own lives and workplace.

Instead of seeing the world only through our own lens, we begin to see it through others' lenses. It's an amazing thing to see the world and workplace through 90% vs. our own 5%. While there is no science behind those numbers, it's a metaphor for how most people view their surroundings, and then the entire universe opens up for us when we engage with and promote diversity.

There is a very simple answer to this: talent and knowledge and practice.

I have stated earlier how a more diverse workplace can bring much more to the work environment than when the workplace is uniform. There is more talent, knowledge, and practice within a diverse workplace.

Think about it from this perspective: When television first started, everything was black and white. The same was true for films. Then color was introduced, and it changed the way in which we view everything. With films, they were not only black and white initially, but they were silent. With "talkies" and with color, it changed the way in which we viewed them.

With greater talent, knowledge, and practice, we are, and will remain, more competitive. Many larger companies now have a DEI (diversity, equity, and inclusion) officer. I think this is a huge step forward and an investment in the organization. Many companies also have a supplier diversity officer, which encourages companies to seek out suppliers that are owned by minorities, women, people of color, and members of the LGBTQ+ community. Making an investment in both of these areas goes a long way toward embracing diversity.

Diversity in the workplace and in our respective organizations more aptly reflects the world around us. When we embrace that view in our own organizations, it not only contributes greatly to our own worlds (including the organizations we are part of), but it also contributes to healing the many divisions we have in our countries, societies, and organizations. It contributes to understanding and to the colorful rainbow of individuals, each one of whom brings something of value to the table, which in many cases can enhance those organizations.

Would you rather watch your TV in black and white or with brilliant colors? Would you rather watch a film with sound and color? I believe the answer is a resounding YES.

HIRE ON MERIT, NOT DIVERSITY

DR. BRUCE RIPPEE

Diversity is a celebration of all that makes the human race unique. Included in that celebration are the life experiences, beliefs, ideas, causes, colors, dreams, emotions, and experiential filters that we bring to social and professional interactions.

The most important part of diversity in the workplace is innovation and vision. I hold the belief that stagnation in any industry is a slow, sure death. The economic and business world keeps changing, and if a business is to thrive, it must evolve with the ebb and flow of political, social, religious, and intellectual pursuits. The business must also reach outside and find a way to connect to unrelated industries and socially important enterprises if it is to remain relevant long enough to become a legacy. If we define our mission as what we do daily and our vision of where the company is going, diversity is vital to that mission.

One of my analogies of ideation is that a group of us from different backgrounds and with different forward-facing dreams and goals sit on white chairs in a completely white room—the walls, floor, and ceiling are all white. In the middle of the circle is a huge vat of spaghetti. At the word "go," we all start throwing handfuls of sticky spaghetti (our ideas) around the room. We have generally made a horrible mess at the end of the session, but somewhere on the walls, ceiling, or floor, there is a work of art, a new path or idea worth time and pursuit. Ideation and innovation require diversity, not only for the throwing of the spaghetti, but also for the recognition of the artistry that can come from different people all dreaming together.

Diversity becomes very important to a good leader due to contact points with the public. Here is an extremely simplistic example: When I first purchased my practice, I believed that I was young, strong, extremely smart, and capable of fixing a rainy day. I had two employees. Anne was about fifty-five years old, heavyset, and what most early 1990s people would call "frumpy," while Jane was twenty, cute, and full of energy. Both of them saw the patients as they came in, and either one would be at checkout when they left. Interestingly, patients always gravitated to one or the other of them. They were recognized as being part of a team, but almost every patient had their favorite, and the reasons for their favoritism varied so greatly that I truly had no idea why.

One day, Martha, a very powerful civic leader, came in to see me at my clinic. I knew that this could be a very good thing for me and my practice, as powerful patients and friends are great for any young doctor. She was referred by an existing patient who was also dealing with the same type of migraine headaches from which Martha suffered. Martha was worth many millions of dollars and was used to some measure of deference. When Jane greeted her, she was joyful, light-hearted, and bouncy. Martha was unimpressed and quietly filled out her paperwork.

And then Anne took her back to my room, at which point Martha told her about her position in the civic council and how many meetings she had to miss to be here and then asked about what I might do, how long it would take, if it would hurt, and so on. In her beautiful, calm, perfectly frumpy way, I heard Anne say, "Honey, Dr. Bruce doesn't care who you are or why you are that. The only thing that I have ever seen him give a crap about is that when you leave here, you are much better than when you came in."

Martha was a true gem when I walked into the room, and solving her problem was very easy for both of us. Jane, as incredible as she was, would not have been able to set a person at ease in that fashion. Thirty years later, Martha continues to refer patients to my clinic. I don't know how well that exchange would have worked if I didn't have Anne, but I doubt that two Janes or another person exactly like me would have worked out nearly as well.

Diversity helps a workplace avoid some problems, especially in businesses with more than twenty-five employees or those in the service industry, because it offers a true cross-section of differing perspectives and connections. One of my professors had extra credit for every exam he gave. "For five percent in extra credit," he would always say with a smile, "what does

P.A.W. mean?" The answer was, "People. Are. Weird." This plays out in business just as it does in most families and friend groups. Due to the ebb and flow of human emotion and perception, it is always possible for employees or customers to get crosswise and have conflict.

One of the best ways that we have found to reduce or mitigate the conflict is to have someone with a similar background and culture speak to the upset employee or customer. If I understand correctly, diversity should not be promoted in the workplace. If we take the definition of promotion as activities that further a cause, work is not the venue for that. The workplace is designed to promote the products or services that further the mission and vision of the enterprise. We should live to celebrate the differences and uniqueness of all human beings and work hard to create a culture of necessity for these traits, but unless the business is directly linked to diversity, promotion would be a mistake.

I always welcome disagreement, but here is my argument. My entire adult life has been based on empowerment to the point that I have two pet peeves: virtue signaling and championing a cause for which I have no understanding or affiliation. In other words, I would no more promote in the workplace that I loved and appreciated heterosexuality than I would homosexuality. Race, creed, gender, political affiliation, and so on have nothing to do with whether a person can do the job that is required of them. That should be the only focus of the workplace. Except for the fact that we need new and differing perspectives, a person's diversity should be a non-factor in a working environment. Can you do the job? Get along with your co-workers? Follow the rules of the business and help our customers receive the best possible result? Yes? You're hired. No? Can you be trained to do the job, get along with your co-workers, and so on? Yes? You're hired. No? There is another opportunity out there for you, but here is a bad fit.

If I promoted those who were considered part of the diversity movement, I would be doing them a disservice. There are markets that expect the virtue signaling of a diverse corporation. In those markets, it is probably necessary to make some type of outward display, but the true champion of a diverse workplace has an "I care so much about you that your diversity is a non-factor for me, and I see the person that you are—not your cause."

No one likes to hear that because we have developed a society of keyboard warriors who like to champion causes for other people as though they aren't capable of sticking up for themselves. In my world and in the culture of my clinic, being a specific race, creed, or sexual orientation has about as much pertinence to the business as being bald, having tattoos, or wearing jewelry. We love, need, and see your worth because you are you, not because you hold a social position or belief.

Many years ago, I was fresh out of college with a degree in English writing. I moved back in with my parents for a year because I knew I was headed to chiropractic university. My mom and dad told me to get a job while I was staying with them and pay a modicum of rent. I am so grateful to them for that. I registered for the last few prerequisites at Missouri State University and got a job as a bouncer for a local bar and nightclub. Every night was hand-to-hand combat with someone trying to prove something by starting a fight. One of the worst fights I was ever in was with a man who had a large gold chain around his neck with a three-inch crucifix attached to it. Pure virtue signal. I think we would all agree his actions and words that night were anything but Christian. He was all about promoting Christianity but seemed to lack the core principles.

There are markets that expect the virtue signaling of a diverse corporation. My advice for leveraging a diverse workforce is to ask for refinement from every employee. I have a document titled "We Can be Better." In that document, it asks for specifics about the problem or situation, and then it asks for solutions. When the executive staff looks over these documents, and a solution is offered, they are praised and then discussed at the next monthly corporate meeting.

The more diverse the workforce, the more likely we are to detect hidden, underlying problems and obtain new and innovative ways to deal with them. It is well known that the act of filling out the "We Can be Better" form is a great way to earn brownie points with the C-suite and get recognized at monthly and annual meetings. I am fortunate to have a unique perspective on diversity since I have pushed for chiropractic diversity and inclusion my entire career. Even though the diversity movement is generally centered around sexual orientation, identity, race, or creed, we have all been marginalized at some point in our lives. I would ask those who have dealt with this to hear my story and see if they can swap out a few words and find a corollary. There is a message here for both the executives and those who are employed as part of the machine that makes the business viable.

I was at a neighborhood party in a beautiful home of a friend whose entire family had come to see me for chiropractic care. I had helped the kids with the strains and sprains of being athletes and the parents with the nicks, dings, and stiffness that stem from a daily life of ten hours a day at the computer. There were about fifty neighbors at this party, half of whom I had never met. I walked downstairs, and Matt, our host, came up to hug me. "Dr. Bruce!" he said, giving me a big manly hug. His wife was only a few feet away and turned to me, also offering a warm hug—a truly gentle, loving human being. Jay was also there, and this big, burly voice that can only come through a magnificent beard yelled over the music, "Dr. Bruce!" Again with a hug. A few more hugs, handshakes, and pats on the back later, and I found myself talking with Shelly—a new graduate from medical school graduate who had interned at my clinic.

A lady I had never met walked up with wide eyes, a big smile, and a glass of wine. "I heard people calling you Dr. Bruce. What kind of doctor are you?" I told her that I was a chiropractor. Her smile melted, and she made a face that looked as though she had just discovered her wine was actually a urine sample. "Oh, God!" she said. "I thought you were a real doctor." She turned away and took about two steps before Shelly, a newly minted MD, lit into her like a young mama bear protecting her (much older) cub. Unfortunately, many other people heard the argument, and some even chose to join in. At that point, I became a mere prop in the background of the scene taking place at a friend's party. That was not what I wanted. We all have the right to speak our truth, and my worth was not dependent upon her.

I believe that the vast majority of us who have been marginalized for any and all reasons do not want to be divisive in any social setting, let alone the workplace. There are a militant few, but most of us would like to be judged by the content of our character and our deeds, as opposed to some longstanding, ignorant, or just unnecessary prejudice. To those who are different, be willing to answer questions and understand that it is as much our job to love the bigot as it is their job to love us. To those who are hiring the diverse, hire on merit and the willingness to show value to the company. Then celebrate the fact that you now have fresh, new, and exciting differences that can be applied to your daily business activities as well as your innovation and ideation. I believe that, as the employer, it is our job to protect the welcoming culture of the business, but it is a mistake to champion any cause that is unrelated to the workplace.

ABOUT THE AUTHOR

Dr. Bruce Rippee is a sought-after speaker, author, supplement formulator, and business development specialist. He spent the last thirty-one years researching and developing techniques that optimize how we sleep, think, eat, and move. His favorite patient is one who asks, "What can I do for myself?"

Innovate Through Diversity

Luba Sakharuk

When I think of diversity, I think of innovation. I remember a particular case study I read as part of a course on business applications of AI and ML. The case study was about when automatic soap dispensers had just come out and how a person with darker skin couldn't get the soap out of it because the sensor did not work. The issue turned out to be in the algorithm. There were no people with dark skin on that innovation team and so this was never even part of testing strategy. Granted, this was many years ago, but it shows just how narrow thinking innovation can be when there is no diversity.

Recently, I was preparing for a keynote in front of hundreds of thousands of people. I was asked to describe in one or two sentences what I thought the most important aspect of my job was. It seemed like an impossible task, given that I was a full-time digital transformation consultant doing many things on all levels of an organization and an entrepreneur, where I wore even more hats. How could I possibly describe it in one or two sentences? I had two months to prepare for the keynote. I thought about what I found the most value in and what was most dear to my heart, what I lived and breathed every day. I thought about what truly mattered when it came to delivering value to customers and innovation. The one line that I ended up putting in my speech was, "When we create environments where all voices are heard and solutions are created collaboratively, our customers get better products."

I practiced and revisited that line a hundred times (at least). I would put it aside for a day or two and then come back to it to see if it still made sense. Now, months later, it still does. If we truly focus on delivering value to our customers, the best way to achieve that is through collaboration, inclusion, and diversity.

I share the following story in one of my books, *How to FYAIL in Digital Transformations*. About a decade ago, an executive complimented me on my leadership skills, I went back to my cubical and searched online for "what do leaders do?" Leadership skills are so essential to our personal growth, to the growth of the people who surround us, and our organization's ability to innovate, that it is essential to continuously improve and challenge our current leadership skills. As Simon Sinek defines it, "A leader's job is not to do the work for others, it is to help others figure how to do it themselves, to get things done and to succeed beyond what they thought possible." Leaders grow other leaders, and by growing people who are different from them, who have different backgrounds, ideas, and strengths, they grow themselves as well.

In the corporate world, we often talk about the importance of a healthy culture, why it's important, and who is accountable for it. A healthy culture is a culture that has psychological safety, which means people are comfortable challenging each other and speaking up. For people to challenge each other, they have to have different ideas. For people to have different ideas, they have to have different backgrounds, experiences, upbringing, and so on. For all of us to grow and for our organizations to grow and for our customers to get innovative solutions for whatever pain they might want to solve, we need to have diversity in our workplace.

As with anything, we need to start with a "why." Why does diversity matter? Ask your employees if they think it does. If they don't see the value in it, then they are likely to resist adopting any changes associated with diversity. Successful change management is about sharing vision and including people in the solution. It works best when you identify those who are ready to embrace change and implement it in their organization. The best way to persuade others to join is by sharing wins and success stories.

To be competitive, you need to innovate, and to innovate, you need engaged employees with creative ideas. As leaders, we need to pay close attention to the people we have. I remember being hired as an expert in agile methodology, and while I was a full-time employee with tons of ideas, the company decided to hire an outside consultant. I remember wondering why they would hire someone else when they didn't even ask me if I had any ideas for improvement? With time, after I felt like my ideas and expertise were not valued, I chose to move on.

After becoming a consultant myself and having an opportunity to engage with hundreds of employees and leaders, I realized that this similar experience happens with many roles and at different levels of an organization. When people are not included and diversity in ideas is not valued, people become disengaged and eventually move on. When businesses lose talent, it for sure doesn't help with innovation or being more competitive.

To embrace anything, we need to have the right mindset in place. We need to understand why what we embrace is important and we need to take action, not just talk about it. We also need to choose the best way to measure success and have feedback loops in place to ensure we can pivot if something we put in place is not moving us toward our goals.

One of the big topics these days is employee retention. There are many articles out there talking about reasons people leave and the cost of rehire. From my personal experience as an employee and also from being on the listening side of the many venting sessions, I can say that many people leave when don't feel like they are being valued. As leaders, we need to be all eyes and ears. We need to invest time in our people and make sure we promote diversity by playing an active role in it. We need to pay attention to who we hire, who we promote, and what we do to promote diversity and inclusion. We also need to put processes in place and clearly communicate company values and goals. If the company is loud and clear that diversity is what the company values and all are held accountable to contribute to that, then the company will have a high chance in achieving diversity and leveraging it for growing, innovating, and bringing the most value to their customers.

Self-reflect regularly to see if your thoughts and actions promote diversity. Ask for feedback, be open to receive feedback, and be willing to give feedback to others if you see that diversity is not being embraced. If we set a goal for ourselves and for our organizations to improve diversity and choose to be intentional, we will succeed in achieving that goal. We must choose to prioritize diversity and inclusion for the sake of our employees and our customers.

ABOUT THE AUTHOR

Luba Sakharuk holds a master's degree in computer science from Worcester Polytech Institute of Technology and started her career as a software engineer. The unique insights and abilities she gained in her career led her to agile coaching, facilitation, training, leadership, and digital transformations. While working full time as a senior lead consultant, she published two books and founded RALM3 Consulting LLC, focusing on public speaking, facilitation, and mentorship.

Dear Entrepreneur,

Are you looking for a way to take your business to the next level? Writing a co-authored book could be the answer you've been searching for.

As an entrepreneur, you know the importance of building an authoritative presence in your industry. When you co-author a book, it adds instant credibility to your name and opens the door to increased influence and networking opportunities.

That's why SAB Publishing is excited to offer you this unique opportunity. Co-authoring a book with us gives you the chance to become a bestselling author and increase your lead flow. Plus, you'll be able to build your brand and grow your business.

At SAB Publishing, we understand the needs of entrepreneurs like you. That's why we make it easy to write a co-authored book with us. An experienced publisher and editor helps you write a compelling story, as well as professional design and marketing services.

Take the first step to becoming a bestselling author and growing your business.

Contact SAB Publishing today (jetlaunch.link/sp) to learn more about our co-authoring opportunities to grow your business.

Chris O'Byrne
SAB Publishing
books@strategicadvisorboard.com

Made in the USA
Monee, IL
09 February 2023

26852611R00075